BOOKS BY W. C. BROWNELL

FRENCH TRAITS
An Essay in Comparative Criticism.

FRENCH ART
Classic and Contemporary Painting and Sculpture.

The Same. Illustrated Edition. With Forty-eight Full-page Plates.

VICTORIAN PROSE MASTERS

AMERICAN PROSE MASTERS

CRITICISM

STANDARDS

THE GENIUS OF STYLE

CHARLES SCRIBNER'S SONS

THE GENIUS OF STYLE

THE GENIUS OF STYLE

BY

W. C. BROWNELL

CHARLES SCRIBNER'S SONS
NEW YORK · LONDON
1924

Printed in the United States of America

TO EDWIN HOWLAND BLASHFIELD

CONTENTS

		PAGE
I.	Order and Movement	1
II.	Manner and Personality	38
III.	The Art of Prose	75
IV.	English Prose Tradition	111
V.	Present-Day Uses—Social and Personal	142
VI.	Present-Day Uses—Art and Letters	181
	Index	219

THE GENIUS OF STYLE

I

ORDER AND MOVEMENT

ONE of the perennial subjects of philosophical discussion, being important, indeterminate, inexhaustible and, above all, intrinsically interesting, style is at the present time as lively a theme as it ever was. The wealth of existing treatment of it, instead of discouraging further consideration, invites and warrants it, by no means possessing in the mass or reaching in the reduction the finality affected in occasional dogmatic detail. At the present time such consideration seems particularly pertinent because the general subject has developed a new phase. Novelty to-day resides in phase rather than in fact and this in itself involves reopening cases already amply adjudicated, since the facts are forgotten and precedents consequently precluded. Everything but axioms calls for re-argument, and even axioms must walk delicately under penalty of being stigmatized as conventions. The phase here in question is the curious coincidence of a rather pointed neglect of style in practice with a frequently exhibited propensity to speculate about it. Books, reviews, lectures, the newspapers discuss it copiously. And though still more curiously the tendency of the time is also theoretically to minimize its significance, to treat it in trituration as a matter of taste and therefore facultative, to reduce it to its lowest terms as an incidental of rhetoric or other technic, to side-step it as a natural gift about which there is no more to be said (however much may be said around it), and finally to deny its existence altogether as the common denominator of its various nevertheless palpable embodiments, this is perhaps due to the inveteracy with which, everywhere, practice seeks to justify itself by theory. And theory once established, practice receives from it reciprocal reinforcement. In practice, assuredly, in spite of much "good writing" as well as less good "fine writing," one rather phlegmatic and the other decidedly febrile, we have no surplusage of intelligently conceived style.

We are thus more and more coming comfortably to ignore in practice and disparage in theory what nevertheless we find it academically interesting to discuss—forgetting to look for it as readers, as observers of æsthetic phenomena in the mass, forgetting as writers, as artists, to make it an aim or an instrument, as a public forgetting to savor it. From this largely passive attitude to active distaste is but a step—a step we have yet to take perhaps before we enter upon the back track of retreat all along the line from the deserts of "listlessness" and "mad endeavor," and "all that is at enmity with joy" to the mapped lands and charted waters of orderly development. Very likely on the other hand we are already on the verge of recoil—the only untried open road to so many among us, and as such, beckoning alluringly, it may be, to the generous spirit of adventure characteristic of the present day. Certain signs may be interpreted to indicate it. But the moment of crisis in movements of this kind is difficult to identify. Apparently, so far as style is concerned, our Canaan is yet in the distance.

Critical analysis, to be sure, has been occupied with the subject of style, probably from the earliest and certainly down to the latest days of its practice hitherto. Naturally, attempts to define it have been numerous and, as usual with perennial subjects, much more numerous than successful. Failures, however, have not been fruitless. They have served to keep the subject alive, and it is a subject profitable to study at least on Lessing's principle of preferring the pursuit to the attainment of truth. The by-products of its pursuit in this instance have been found interesting or the pursuers would have been fewer. Erasmus, indeed, remarked that every definition was a misfortune; and one can see how, amid the rigid formulations of the letter that killeth in which the sixteenth century endeavored to fix the spirit that giveth life, a humane and expansive temperament should find injurious as well as irksome the prevailing mania of defining the indefinable. Still, there is something so thoroughly satisfactory about the capture of one of the elusive sprites that people the air of the critical imagination, in order to confine it within a compass narrow enough for contemplating comfortably, that it is small wonder their pursuit should be popular—that so many, less impatient than Pilate regarding a similar quest, after asking what one of these radiant appearances really is, should "stay for an answer." The reason why the definition of style is so difficult is perhaps because style is a universal element, an ultimate that enters into combination and characterizes compounds without itself having any organization particular enough to particularize—one that may be tested for and identified but not delimited nor detached.

What, however, we cannot define we can often

describe. Have you not, in fact, observed that what eludes definition is apt to accumulate description in proportional luxuriance? Such description may occasionally be even more illuminating than a definition—especially an imperfect one. To call anything an ultimate, for example, is a kind of vague definition, narrowing the field of examination and a check on loose thinking, but to do so is clearly to convey a less vivid idea of it than a comprehensive description may succeed in doing—most of our knowledge being, I suppose, phenomenal rather than essential. In any case, it seems a useful preliminary in considering, however approximately, this shyest of the sprites I spoke of to fix at the outset its status as an ultimate æsthetic factor, legitimately figuring in various fields of mental activity and entering into combinations for which it has innate affinities—not only in art and letters, but in the discipline of thought and the conduct of life.

The spirit of style at all events, if not the secret, we can have no difficulty in recognizing—as to distinguish music from mere sound it is needless to know its vibrational idiosyncrasy. When Henry James remarks of Lowell that his career was in the last analysis "a tribute to the dominion of style"; that this is the idea that to his sense Lowell's name "most promptly evokes"; and that "he carried style, the style of literature, into regions in which we rarely look for it," no one is in any doubt as to what he means. But as to the value of it or the practicality of preaching it we are decidedly more sceptical. And it seems to me that if we considered a little more closely and extensively this abstraction which we recognize when we see its operation and effect but in general consider either casually or unsympathetically, its substantial interest should more clearly appear. We may do so in the case of Henry James himself, whose work Mr. Stuart Sherman defines as concentratedly devoted to the æsthetic element in life—with the interesting result, by the way, of winning, under sharp reservations on other counts, his critic's "adoration"; which shows how far the liberal Puritan partisan may go when he enters the pagan province of pure beauty. I dare say he is quite right, though a little of the discomfort inherent in suggested readjustments attended in my case the reading of his brilliant essay. The business of characterizing Henry James looks particularly difficult, perhaps, after one has tried it, but at any rate he seemed somehow more than that—to have more than a purely æsthetic title. An American, almost automatically, winces a little at any serious aggrandizement of the æsthetic element—no doubt obscurely obeying the instinct of self-preservation and feeling safer with the beauty of holiness than with the holiness of beauty. Keats's devotion to "the principle of beauty in all things" and his complete identification of beauty with truth have for us the poetic sanction; in the poetic sense the most appalling, the most repellent truth looks at us—very likely more than at more sensuous æstheticians—with an expression of beauty that is due solely to its truth which, incontestably, we prize as greatly as others. But poetry has hitherto been for us a thing apart and though quite recently it seems to have taken the place of religion, once similarly commended to be "carried into our daily life," its principles have not been accorded general authority, not having, in fact, shared the spread of its practice.

There is obviously, however, an æsthetic element both in literature and art in general and in life itself that is very much to be reckoned with, an element of whose existence and authority Mr. Sherman strikingly reminds us in ascribing a rather exclusive preoccupation with it to so undoubted a master as Henry James. And of this comprehensive element of life and letters, recognized universally as æsthetic, a marked constituent, however defined and however depreciated, is the style that James noted in all the activities of Lowell. It is quite possible, I think, to contend that, ideally speaking, style is its informing constituent. For that matter style lies more or less latent in any constituent that informs anything.

"Listening in" recently at one of those family exchanges of literary gossip conducted by our columnists and now so popular, I was surprised at the mention of a poetess known in her day as the Sweet Singer of Michigan, a sort of "find" in some antiquarian excavation by the writer. I recall the rollicking chorus of a poem by this lady chanting what now might be viewed as the forerunner of a then new gospel in the adjuring words: "Leave off the agony, leave off style!" She may have had in mind the cakewalk and its stylistic congeners in which we get the raw article and observe the informing spirit in its excess rather than at its best, but she was clearly an inspirationist and a partisan of the bald despatch now regnant and what she resented was the taking of thought involved in "putting on" (as it used to be called) the style which she implored us to leave off. Her plea has triumphed in this fulness of time. We have quite generally left it off. Undoubtedly a realist, she but anticipated the current impatience of the artificial even in the good sense of the word, style being undeniably in this sense as artificial a force in the day of realism as when in periods less inhospitable to it, whether classic, academic, or romantic, it has exercised the nevertheless not valueless function of bringing order out of chaos.

That at any rate is in no small part what style does. How, more precisely, may it be described? Few writers have become so identified with a subject so general in its nature as Buffon has with style. His discourse is a model exposition and has made of its author the most cited authority on its theme, nowhere else, perhaps, treated with the same explicitness or more suggestion, in more varied detail or with greater breadth of view. No wiser point of departure could be chosen than his statement that style is "nothing other than the order and movement which we put into our thoughts." The first three words—"nothing other than"—which make the statement a definition are perhaps inexact, and consequently to that extent the statement may be faulty. But to the admirable description that follows they are superfluous. Style may not be merely the order and movement that we put into our thoughts but it is at least that—if something more not something other. It does not reside in the thoughts themselves, and it is lacking in their expression in proportion as this is either disorderly or static. As abstractions order and movement are entitled to every respect; one could hardly praise them too highly. Recognized vaguely perhaps rather than realized fully as "Heaven's first law," order acquires a more definite dignity in Senancour's classification of it, as an essential part of our inclinations, with our twin basic instincts of self-preservation and reproduction, in a phrase which Arnold uses as an epigraph to "Literature and Dogma." Yet, as Fénelon observed, it is the rarest of qualities in the works of the mind; so difficult is it to realize the most inherent of ideals. Movement, in any case, is essentially life itself. The two combined constitute the formative element of an æsthetic composition and in a real sense thus the art of art. Therefore while, considered as order and movement, style can hardly be conceived concretely as a compositional part of the substance it qualifies, it may be abstracted from this as an element—not a created feature but a constructive factor, integral not incidental. It may most profitably, I think, be considered as that factor of a work of art which preserves in every part some sense of the form of the whole. An informing spirit running through a composition, a theme through variations, it realizes relations as well as formulates statements and is the agent that organizes variety into unity. It is, in truth, the organic factor in art of any kind, the factor in virtue of which every part of any whole becomes at once a means and an end, each detail contributory as well as in itself significant. There is nothing abstruse or recondite about this description. Everyone who has ever put together a puzzle picture has only to imagine its parts possessed of some individual interest in order to comprehend an organism, or for that matter need only consider his own anatomy. More briefly one may say that a work of art possesses style when the detail, counting in itself, also contributes to the general effect. In consequence of this, coherence and interdependence, continuity and harmony, become salient traits of the work as a whole, whatever it be, a sentence or a treatise, a sonnet or a symphony, a still-life or a landscape, a coin or a monument.

The genius of style, therefore, is easily discriminated from that of mere individual expression, of which cogency and energy or other personal traits are conspicuous characteristics. Concentration on the intrinsic interest of any detail tends naturally to a diversion if not to the discord which is integrally hostile to style, however it may compensate for supplanting it by emphasizing the energy of expression. It may indeed compromise with style in an *entente* of mutual modification and reinforcement. Discord assuredly has its uses—even in music. Meanwhile during discord, as a rule style marks time. The genius of style, which remembers and anticipates in the act of expression (thus automatically enriching expression with added values), which, within the limits of harmony modifies the native form of the concrete individual thing it is stating with reference both to what has preceded and to what is to follow it, is silenced oftenest in the presence of what is in excess independent and idiosyncratic, even eccentric by contrast. The two are as distinct as our old friends objective and subjective—whose labels respectively, in point of fact, they wear—but should accord as complements. Nothing could be less individual than the operation of the genius of style. Consciousness recognizes it, I think, as belonging to the domain of the not-ourselves. And analysis confirms consciousness as to the external character of its agency in influencing for either restraint or impetus even the internal operation of any compositional effort, however individual, that it directs and controls. A virtual analogy is furnished by Nature herself ceaselessly at work in harmonizing the object with its environment and abhorring in her orderly evolution "sports" almost as much as vacuums. Sports do, of course, occur in style as in nature, but only after they have "bred true" long enough to lose their sport character does their progeny establish its title to the rôle of type and exemplar. Meantime the pressure of both natural law and the genius of style is constant. There is no logical step to be taken between denying the universality of style as a principle and affirming as fact the phenomena of its operation—which does not always prevent the taking of an illogical one. "The lion on the flag," says the Persian poet, "is but a painted lion, but in the wind it moves and marches." Quite as real and similarly dynamic in its invisible agency is the spirit of style.

That it should be negated or vilipended by the spirit—or rather, let us say, in view of its character, the temper—of the present day is logical enough, the key-note of the day being not so much expression, even, as self-expression; nothing objective can very well attract the egoistic complex. But I suspect that the hostility or indifference to style as generally understood is inveterate rather than altogether transitional and arises from a misconception of it as connoting not a principle of art but the prescription of some method. Perhaps it is reasonable that in a time when so many teach not only should there be so few that learn but that there should also be so general a revolt against the didactic. It is possibly imagined that to celebrate style is to inculcate an ideal of self-suppression with, inherently, sinister designs on the freedom of the individual—the individual who nowadays is more disposed than a generation that admired Poe more temperately, to echo Poe's avowal: "My whole nature utterly revolts at the idea that there is any being in the Universe superior to myself." Possibly when style is commended, or even encountered, the traditional, the classic, the consecrated are discerned behind the mask, and style which, it is true, does suggest these categories of the conventional, as they have come to be more or less widely and very conventionally considered, incurs the obloquy of the company it keeps. The individual is however, in any case, needlessly concerned. He is in no danger from the professors, of whom a very considerable and articulate radical contingent—the pedants of progress they might perhaps be called, not too paradoxically—are on his side and themselves prescribe liberty in large doses, perhaps for the same reason that their predecessors preached restraint, namely, to meet general expectations. Style would perhaps have fewer enemies if it were more universally understood that, though a universal principle which could only salutarily enter into any composition of real importance, it has no means of intruding where it is not wanted, since it must wait to be invited; that, even if more of a virus than a virtue, it would be insignificant as a menace to the deliberately casual and designedly miscellaneous; and that, like other abstractions, it has no concrete "norm" of excellence which *could* be prescribed as a formula for introducing order and movement into the most disorderly and deadlocked of chaotic cases. It does, indeed wherever manifest preach by example. But it has neither a system nor a method involving conformity to any particular programme, and the sceptical practitioner born again in its spirit would probably feel possessed of a new instrument of expression instead of fettered with old chains—with results in time not displeasing to the most unconventional.

For the effect of the spirit of style in a work of art is precisely to add wings to it. The effect of following any objective ideal is elevation. Uplift means first of all getting out of one's self. It appeals in this way to the imagination as adventure does. But it also involves what adventure does not, definite aspiration rather than vague enthusiasm. And this aspiration to achieve rather than to experience, to reach a goal rather than to explore the unknown, to attain the normal rather than invent the novel, springs from perceiving the existence in the ideal sphere of a quality for which we have no other word so apt as perfection. Perfection in any work of art implies correspondence with the standard set by its ideal. It is accordingly something external and universal, something which one may more rationally swear allegiance to than set out to subvert. Compared with the expression of restive personal feeling, revolutionary enthusiasm, the satisfaction of natural impulse—to all of which original conception owes so much—the pursuit of perfection in technical execution is artificial, or, at least, unlike the "profuse strains" of the skylark's "art," premeditated. It involves the discipline and restraint, as well as guidance and instruction, necessary to secure conformity to the *laws* of perfection. Artistic aspiration, indeed, is rather for law than for fact. It seeks a secret of which it has preliminarily felt the need and perceived the operation and which it would make its own—the secret of grouping, governing, and directing such experiences and imaginings as it has already had, in such a way as to endue them with the coherence of character.

This secret is, in fact, the secret of creative art. Through its possession the creative artist creates—his own character to begin with. Some ideal connected with duty, decorum, ambition, or at any rate consistency, welds his impulses and hesitations, his tendencies and inhibitions into an individuality that counts for itself apart from the sum of these. By giving rein to natural impulse a certain character may be acquired, a certain course run, but we may be sure that without a certain constraint converging the vagrom variations of natural impulse toward the accent and emphasis of a unified entity —intimations of which are recognizable all along the chain of the acts and words that compose it—not even such distinction as that of Alcibiades or Alva can be attained, to say nothing of exemplary examples. As Arnold, in one of his most fundamental essays, cites Cicero as saying, man alone of created beings has an impulse to establish some other law to control the law of his nature, and this impulse to exteriorize our effort in accord with some ideal that we feel to be universal—the *lingua franca* of elevated endeavor—and constraining us on the hither side of impertinent self-assertion, may quite justifiably be called the artistic as distinguished from the natural impulse. It is unlikely that in the sphere of æsthetics either abstract or technical—

where I have heard a new moulding has long been sought in vain—the most enthusiastic innovator will invent many additions to the laws of perfection. But if his curiosity can be aroused he may perhaps discover those already ascertained and hitherto held in honor; and he may perhaps end by feeling their force. And in all activity that is at all sustained the influence which chiefly imposes upon the operation of the artistic impulse the direction and guidance of the laws of perfection, to the end of abiding interest and authority, is the spirit that unifies it in harmony and vivifies it in rhythm—the spirit of style. "The bust outlasts the throne; the coin, Tiberius," in virtue of their art, but their art survives in virtue of its style. The bust of Julian, the coin of Justinian survive as documents.

Under the influence of style the mechanism of rhetoric, the picture's lines and masses, the sculptor's planes and profiles, the architect's thrusts and supports, *pleins et vides*, function organically and the interrelations of parts count as structural members of the larger whole. And while engaged in transaction of this quality, and especially of this difficulty, though sustained by his sense of the beauty of the result if successful, the artist's concentration upon his task of realizing his ideal is likely to monopolize his attention—at any rate, to the exclusion of egoistic impulse. I remember a remark of Quincy Ward's that has always seemed to me particularly illuminating. We were speaking of purpose in art. "If it's a work of any importance," said Ward, "I fancy the artist is fully occupied in trying to pull it off." Truly. And the artist thus absorbed is—ultimate purpose already formed and elementary difficulties overcome—in proportion to his own seriousness occupied with the style of his work, its order and movement, its unity in variety, its stream of harmonious but accented continuity, its totality of effect. He is absorbed, I should imagine, in feeling and executing this complicated but fascinating task in a kind of controlled excitement and directed purpose, endeavoring to embody his ideal of how the subject should be treated as well as in love with the subject itself. Indeed, his treatment is part of the subject, and as art has been called the interpenetration of the object with its ideal, style may be taken as that of the treatment with *its* ideal, with which also he is in love. In the widest sense, thus, style would be the art of technic, that element of technical expression which makes an art of what otherwise is at best but skill.

It is particularly salient in sculpture, in which

style is often as clearly marked as *a* style in architecture. Often, indeed, sculpture succeeds so well in expressing its defining idiosyncrasy, in being sculpture, that it is nothing else; so well, that is, that its style is the first and last thing about it. Everyone knows Bartholomé's beautiful tomb at Père Lachaise. Boutet de Monvel, praising it to me once, remarked: "It's not sculpture, but it's art." He meant perhaps that it was too personal for so abstract an art. Its style is in some degree subverted to its personal expression, which is indeed poignant enough to justify its excursus from the prescription of its own canons. On the other hand, even a great decorative genius like Jean Goujon expresses himself chiefly, perhaps, in elements of surface and contour, design and pattern, conceived as factors of pure style. The material of sculpture is so uncompromisingly, so defiantly, concrete that its art becomes correspondingly abstract. The perfect union of the two elements prevailing in the Periclean epoch has been difficult to recapture. Personal expression in it often gets little farther than the style thus imposed by the art itself. The academic sculpture of France is condemned for this reason by a vigorous personality like Rodin, but it is in its own way delightful in consequence of its possession of this delightful æsthetic element. Chapu and Dubois get successfully far away from the palpability of their material into a region where what counts most is the generalized effect of style. "*Faut voir le profil,*" is, I believe, the constantly reiterated injunction of the sculptor-instructors at the Beaux-Arts, and certainly no one could succeed in sculpture who did not constantly bear the outline in mind. This unremitting checking of the detail by the contour secures its correspondence to the *ensemble*—secures style, in a word. Any undue individual accent thus appears as a jar, and the whole composition is modelled by the details functioning as forces, of which the whole is the actual resultant as well as ideally the origin. Nothing accordingly can be a better demonstration of the value as well as the character of style than any merely competent example of this highly abstract yet concretely tactile art. Everyone realizes that to call anything sculptural is to credit it with style.

But the same is true of all the visual arts. Reflection would supply endless instances which in illustrating common principles perform for these the service of a diagram in a demonstration. In Raphael's "Saint Cecilia," a signal as well as superb example of style, it has been remarked by a romantic critic that the figures "pose well."

They do. If they did not the large canvas they fill would lose its style. They are few in number and stand absorbed in listening to the celestial choiring above them, an act which is only suggested action and which relaxing their pose would stultify. The movement is concentrated and, as in general with Raphael—always, in the sense of exemplifying the spirit of style—spiritualized. The same is true of the miniature "Vision of Ezekiel," in which, though the interrelation of the figures is tranquil, the whole remarkable group is in animated action. Almost everything of Fra Bartolommeo, whose sense of style may very well have quickened Raphael's undoubtedly congenital endowment, has the same kind of effect—the effect of presenting to the beholder the idea of style as well as the subject of the picture. The beautiful "Visitation" of his friend Albertinelli has it, too, in a distinguished degree. So, too, does Andrea del Sarto's masterpiece, the "Madonna del Sacco," with an even greater simplification, the movement being so blandly pictorial as to secure an agreeable equilibrium unmarked by either stasis or emphasis of direction. In Donatello's "Judith," a composition in which his art most clearly sublimates his material and expresses his idea with a stiff singleness austerely detached from any but purely artistic feeling for the tragic subject, movement is suggested still more strongly by arrested action. Such works are supreme examples of style, not only because of their abstract order and movement, but because their order and movement are the means through which in a supreme degree the spirit of style animates their concrete representation. In all the larger elements there is an intimation—not indeed an image—of the whole, and as it were a consciousness of subserving the general effect rather more than of displaying individual character; beside the explicitness of the *ensemble* its elements seem almost incidental.

Less illustrious and more general illustrations are as exact. A play of any length without the larger relations of acts would merely assemble successive detail. The architect who conceives design as pattern, or his art as decorated planning, is lost—an articled apprentice to the prince of this world. A picture without mass values would (if well done) count ocularly as a Persian rug. The more detail, the greater the miscellaneity calling for simplification into organic relation. The composer who, like Debussy, composes relations only, without letting us miss the missing parts, achieves pure style if not "absolute music." The Claude Lorrain mirror puts style into the landscape, the kaleidoscope puts it into a few bits of glass. It is the spirit of style that transmutes life into art. Madame Sans Gêne must rather conspicuously have lacked it, but it is as certain that Madame Réjane did not. Formality has indubitably more than freedom, the pictorial more than the picturesque, the race-horse more than the runaway, the piston more than the flail, the flight of the swallow more than the flutter of the fledgling. It is what keeps artistic forces in play or in poise, but always free of stagnation. "As you were" subtracts style from the activity of drill. A masterpiece mutilated has plainly lost its perfection, but as plainly, though not of course as fully, preserves its style. A note struck on the piano is style-less; the pedal supplies style; the chord still more. It is the sense of style that stiffens the soldier under the drill-sergeant's command: "Attention!"; that makes a walk a march; that attends the change from the trot to the canter. And inevitably it exacts tension, whatever the suavity of the effect. The actor representing relaxation may not aimlessly slouch or sprawl.

The tension of style—or what the French call *tenue*—is needed to make emotion count—that is, for anyone but the actor, writer, orator, singer himself. If the artist does it all, none gets to the audience save as spectacle. Appreciative perception in the house cannot participate with uncontrolled susceptibility on the stage; the spectator must merely absorb its display, like blotting-paper. When the true artist feels anything so fundamentally and persistently as, thinking of it and not of himself, to regard it impersonally instead of egoistically, he tends to poetize it, to express it with a detached sense of form consonant with its dignity. Depth of feeling, purified of transitory intensities, finds style, thus, a natural reliance for elevated expression. In the preface to his "Last Poems," Mr. Housman speaks of the "continuous excitement" under which most of his early ones were written. The words happily describe one of the conditions under which works eminent for their style, like Mr. Housman's poems, have in general been successfully composed. No depth of feeling can be too great for the pertinence of this condition to a work of art. In "In Memoriam," for instance, the grief of bereavement, half assuaged, is transmuted into the continuous excitement of endeavoring adequately to express it in consonance with its dignity of origin and its depth. This is the normal process in elegy. The mind at first overborne, struggles out of its paralysis into effusion, but effusion too exalted for purely personal expression, which would, however sincere, be too incoherent for communication or even for relief. Therefore it seeks almost automatically the objective constraints of style. The elegist must "know himself to sing and build the lofty rhyme." Nothing melts us like nobility of thought caught up into style. Nobility stirs us more exquisitely than exquisiteness. Imagination, however sympathetic, warms us but superficially compared with the high disinterestedness of personal detachment exhibited in impersonal exaltation. This moves us like music that strings the sensibility taut and affirms its capacity for forgetfulness of self. Style, in fine, has a play of interrelations and a sustained rhythm, when in combination with adequate substance, that stanch the personal preoccupation of self-pity and stimulate the generous fervor of self-abandonment to the ideal. Exaltation, indeed, is so different from, as to be practically the converse of, the currently so much admired ecstasy, which Mr. Arthur Machen would make the characterizing trait of great, as distinguished from merely interesting, literature—the ecstatic Dickens in this way outshining the photographic Thackeray. Curious conclusion for a stylist, even an ecstatic one.

The sense, less sensitive with ourselves than the sensibility, nevertheless readily responds to pain or pleasure, as the case may be, produced by the various phenomena belonging in the domain of style. The staccato note and the drawl, born one of impulse and the other of vacuity, are equally displeasing as equally without style. Monotony is its negation, lacking the interactions of which it is the emphasis. There is no emphasis so complete, so conclusive, so effective as the synthesis that style involves. The periodic sentence has inevitably and obviously an effect of style which the loose sentence lacks. Perhaps that is the reason it has so generally disappeared. The German prose sentence, being invariably periodic—with its established sequence of "subject, first part of the predicate, object, adverb (time, place, action), second part of the predicate"—has the totality of style, but style reduced to routine, the prolonged and regular iteration of which a caricaturist might almost recover in the Prussian goose-step. Both illustrate style as petrified by system. German poetry is so much another affair than German prose largely because its style is not mechanical. A style may certainly be marked without being marked by style—a truth haply concealed from the wise and prudent but notoriously revealed to tailors, who simply would not stand for qualities often tolerated in letters and art. I remember an experience related with much gusto by an eminent New Yorker of past days who in London on some occasion presented the obligatory letter of introduction to the still more eminent and obligatory Poole. Poole looked at his coat with great contempt, and threw it aside with contumely. "What's the matter with it?" asked Marbury. "No life in it," returned the artist, who knew style-less style when he saw it. Perhaps style may be considered as vivification. At least in any work where it is altogether lacking the lifelessness of the work acquires additional relief.

In thus quickening the composition, the genius of style operates through a fusion of order and movement so intimate that separating the two strands often eludes quantitative analysis. It does not matter, if we recognize them in combination, converged upon their work of vitalizing the parts by permeating them with a sense of the whole, and thus giving everywhere the feeling of completeness, of forces in the repose of equipoise in contrast to stagnation or even stasis. The element of order is most apparent wherever the order is most conspicuously organic. In Lemaitre's characterization of Maupassant, for instance, as: "Author well-nigh irreproachable, in a kind of writing that is not," the last words endue the sentence with style, as it were, under our eyes, recalling without repeating the first ones and thus making a complete organic whole of interdependent parts with a happy economy of means. Lemaitre is habitually happy in this way, establishing his relations not only in epigram but in sustained composition, and giving them a certain inevitability which minimizes them as transitions. It is true, however, that mass counts more largely than line, juxtaposition than interweaving. Articulations have at least more energy than obscure transitions. Lemaitre quarrels with those of Brunetière, who, he says, is as careful to make his transitions plain as others are to disguise them. No doubt to so fluid a writer as Lemaitre Brunetière's seem to dislocate the style. And if Brunetière had possessed the native grace and charm of his critic, whose style achieves its effect through curves and waves, one may say, rather than through the fretted chain of closer-woven logic, he might no doubt have marked his transitions less emphatically. Yet one can but feel that Lemaitre had something to learn from the sharpnesses of his less romantic contemporary, though if the detail of his thought had greater definition we should perhaps, having perceived more quickly and remembering more distinctly, re-read him less often—whereby we should be the losers in the end. One may make the same remark of Sainte-

Beuve's celebrated "sinuosity," also so plain and so attractive a feature of his style as to replace greater organic accent of which I for one, I confess, should occasionally be glad, none the less. And in any case, imperceptible, the value of transitions as an element of style is sacrificed unless such personal force and charm as Lemaitre's or such play of illumination as Sainte-Beuve's replace them. Obviously they emphasize the strand of order, rendering it more clearly organic.

At the same time organic order blends insensibly into movement under the influence of the spirit of style which of mere concatenation makes a current. Doubtless order is nature's and art's as well as Heaven's first law. It is certainly a first necessity in composition. As the English judge observed, pointing out its desirability to confused counsel presenting a case chaotically: "Any kind will do; take the alphabetical if you like." Yet order without movement is hardly conceivable in style of any moment, and indeed it is only when movement supervenes and rhythm undulates through harmony that its character as style becomes clear. Movement discloses the growth instead of merely marking the phases of a composition, defines the directing line of development and emphasizes the unity of the grand construction in lieu of lingering over purely decorative tags and tinsel. Rhythm has not only the intrinsic value of quasi-musical quality, as organic order has that of completeness, of perfection. It is also compositional, and the interplay of its elements may very well express mere equilibrium and none the less have the value of continuity within the composition, already organically disposed. And this sense of continuity resident in rhythm is rhythm's chief stylistic contribution. It prolongs the mood, colors it with repose, security, and permanence, and guarantees it against the shock of discord and distortion, against uneasiness and uncertainty. Poe's poetry, for instance, as also his important prose, is saturated with the sense of continuity, and his philosophy of brevity was doubtless due to the difficulty of sustaining indefinitely the tone he made so pervasive and the mood he made so intense. Mrs. Bacon's "Sons of Sleep," beginning with nature and rising through man to "the great and tireless Heart of all," prolonging the vibration of a single string with stanzaic nodes, is thus a remarkable piece of sustained symmetry and significance as well—a veritable passport to Parnassus, which alas! she visits with unaccountable infrequency.

The more miscellaneous the illustrations one instances the more illustrative: a child practising on the piano and, on making an error, beginning over again, *da capo*, betrays a vague feeling for style by clinging to continuity. It is the sense of continuity that prolongs the skater's glide, the dancer's swing, that tempts the tyro to sway in singing, that leads the orator to eke out his words with flowing gesture, that makes everyone in citing the last clause of the Gettysburg address stress senselessly the "of" in "of the people," that made Lincoln himself "loath to close" the First Inaugural without the moving sweep of style that ends it, that makes the clinging endings of Beethoven so noteworthy that Mr. Henderson devotes a lecture to them. Of course, suggested, as well as actual, context furnishes continuity and is in itself an increment of style. And though in this way the sense is extended beyond the limits of such units as the phrase, the paragraph, and the page, indeed beyond the limits of the entire composition, it is hardly fanciful, I think, to ascribe to this sense of continuity—more or less in subconsciousness, at least, if not explicitly realized—the phenomena of style that are due to association and even to what we know as atmosphere. Both association and atmosphere continue the rhythm into the mental confines of a reader sensitive to such reverberations. Both deeply affect also, if at times they do not originate, the mood, which is such a powerful adjunct of art in producing its effect. Atmosphere anticipates as association recalls. In Musset's comedies the atmosphere is heralded at the outset and to an extent that unifies and even inspires, yet is as independent as an envelope of, the subsequent detail, which appears almost as the result rather than the reason of the atmosphere. The first scene of "On ne badine pas avec l'amour" establishes the tone of the piece as the twang of the tuning-fork the pitch of the song.

Brevity is no bar to style. The words, "Said Abner:" coming at the outset of Browning's "Saul," a piece of style if there ever was one, share by anticipation the vibrations they set going by their position and inversion. The style of sentences like "Jesus wept," "Felix trembled," Keats's "Cold pastoral," Arnold's (of Keats) "He is; he is with Shakespeare," relies, of course, on the continuity of the immediate context, but it also derives from the echo which, after the physical effect has ceased, its reverberations awake in the reader's associated memories. Through association and atmosphere even single words sustain thought and prolong feeling, and are thus factors of style. Indeed this is largely what makes style of diction. After John Bright, during the Crimean War, had profoundly stirred the Commons by declaring that the Angel of Death hovered over them and they had only to listen to hear the beating of his wings, an opponent observed: "If you had said 'flapping' we should have laughed." Ruskin's "writhed columns" cheat the romantic till Mr. Beerbohm's "twisted pillars" make their meretriciousness manifest. The growing substitution of "me" for "I" in the predicate after the verb "to be" is a trifle that betrays the modern leaning toward the prosaic. Prose becoming pedestrian naturally lays aside the stilts of style. Perhaps French, the prose tongue *par excellence*, for this reason is the only tongue whose grammar imposes this usage. "I," of course, connoting the originator and "me" the object, the former possesses the greater dignity. "It is me, be not afraid," would outdo the Revised Version in taking the style out of the Authorized, and color the text with Arianism at once. The rubric followed by his tribe in their most solemn religious service, as described by Friday's father to Robinson Crusoe, which consisted in the ascent of a high mountain and the exclamation "Oh!" connotes an entire chapter on ceremonial style, and certainly is false local color for savagery. Even the change of a single letter may heighten stylistic color. I remember a manuscript correction by Stevenson substituting the "i" for the "u" in "spurt," and capitally illustrating the sensitiveness to the spirit of style for which he early became so famous.

Coleridge's reference, regarding Dante—perhaps the artist of all others supreme in style—to "that soul of universal significance in a true poet's composition in addition to the specific meaning," notes another extension of association through which overtones become audible. The strain in which they, too, blend, thus reinforced with the suggestion of a greater whole, unifies the specific statements of the text as parts, phases, states, and stages of a new and larger completeness. This phenomenon is probably felt oftener than it is analyzed, but there can be few appreciative observers who have not noted, as determining factors of their æsthetic judgments in any of the seven arts, their impressions as to the power and quality of the author of any specific work gained from what the work itself has adumbrated rather than directly disclosed. And these impressions are cardinal. "I am so constituted," says Sainte-Beuve, "that the intellectual form and the character of their authors preoccupy me more than the aim of the works themselves"—profound and searching declaration of the first of literary critics, however simple the formula may seem, and one that puts its finger on the most intimate and indispensable and at the same time far reaching and therefore most richly rewarding interest among the many that solicit the scrutiny of the student, not to say the mere spectator, of the drama staged upon the æsthetic scene. What else could the artist do, what else is he? one asks in the presence of the work itself.

His attitude toward style certainly in part provides the answer. Nothing else indicates so plainly the elevation of the ideal and impersonal aim and inspiration, as nothing else shows so fully whether or no the artist's material is under his control. Too much may undoubtedly be made of style, too disproportionate homage paid to it. Divorced from the pressure of substance it betrays that insipid effect of pedantry parading as power which stamps the mind behind the work as mediocre. As Rodin once exclaimed, "At the Institute they have formulas for sentiments!" Style sterilized, however, is still style and exposes the weakness of its associated substance rather than its own. Without it some of the French *universitaires*, counting for nothing else, would not count at all. To make too little of it, to neglect and decry it, as clearly involves a lack of that development in virtue of which the artist rises out of his own temperamental impulses far enough to measure these impulses by, and permeate them with, those universal and ultimate forces which have inspired, and informed, the outstanding historic achievements consecrated as exemplars of expression by the common consciousness of mankind.

II

MANNER AND PERSONALITY

How the artist subjectively handles—or neglects—the objective element of style is *his* style. Obviously we use the word in two senses, and it has thus a certain ambiguity which in discussion of the general subject it is useful to avoid. Ambiguity of language is perhaps the subtlest of the foes of clearness and in this case it is an especial source of error because the same word is used not only for two different but for two antithetical ideas, at least for one of general and the other of particular application. A number of years ago, accordingly, in writing of French art, in which the objective and impersonal element is so prominent, and having necessarily to distinguish between the two, I ventured for convenience of analysis to substitute for "style" used in the subjective and personal sense the word "manner." The value of an ingenuity of one's own, however, is always suspect; the chances are so numerously in favor either of the need of it being less real than fancied, or of its having long before been tried and found wanting—or, as is also, alas! quite possible, tried and adopted without one's being aware of it, ingenuities often turning out ingenuous. Then, too, though one is quite sure that, aside from dispelling confusion in certain cases, aside from conveying a specific meaning, necessarily specified if it is to be conveyed, "manner" is a better word than "style" for anything so unsystematic and capricious as personal expression, one must, on the other hand, recognize the possibility that the use of "manner" for such personal expression as happens itself to be informed with the spirit of "style" may tend to obscure that important fact. Altogether the subject is surrounded with difficulties, and I was only too glad if I could succeed in expressing an undeniably important distinction, without mooting the matter of justifying the expression. In these circumstances, nevertheless, it was comprehensibly agreeable quite recently to come across Sainte-Beuve's use of the word in substantially the same sense; one had so much rather be right than original!—having incidentally rather a better chance in so wishing of being original into the bargain. In an early notice of Mignet's history of the Revolution, Sainte-Beuve proceeds at once, he says, "to judge the writer's manner." This he declares "dictated by the nature of his talent." "Applied to the French Revolution," he continues, "the manner of M.

Mignet, to say nothing of the seductive and striking qualities which it possesses in itself," finds a congenial subject. And when later he comes to speak of Mignet's style he characterizes it in abstract terms as "much less facile and sonorous than energetic, original, and constantly faithful to the thought behind it, to which it owes everything, both qualities and defects, which is vigorous and complex, fertile in manifold relations embraced in a marvellous symmetry, and which it represents and paints visually by the severe organization of its forms and by the regular mechanism of its balance." One could hardly indicate more clearly without precisely saying so that it is the manner which is "the man," and that the order and movement with which he endues his thoughts constitute his style. And of Mignet's style, as thus understood, he says one would be tempted at first to deem it too "studied." Obviously "studied" is an attribute of style. The "manner" due to the "nature of one's talent" if studied would not be style but affectation.

Of course some distinction in kind between style and manner, if valid, could hardly fail of frequent recognition and must often have been noted without being analyzed. For example, the late Maurice Hewlett, who had a remarkable feeling for both style and distinctions, speaks of Cobbett as having "not a manner but a style," and declares that "Carlyle had manner rather than style, as Emerson, as Meredith." But to feel a distinction is not to determine what it is. Without analysis one may recognize the fact of anything and still miss its character. And to distinguish it in combination—here the end in view—it is essential to know its character. It is not a question of categories but of qualities—the qualities that categories but classify without characterizing. Some of the most interesting simply will not fit into a category—Cobbett's, perhaps, but certainly not Carlyle's. And for the analytical purposes germane in the circumstances the word "manner" is useful to designate one of the two elements of which an individual's style is composed—that is, if it repays analysis—the other being the objective and exterior element of style which his manner modifies into what we call *his* style. Only, in speaking of his style it should be borne in mind that it is thus composite. The whole matter has more than a dialectic interest and is important for this reason, that dwelling exclusively on the purely individual factor in any work of art obscures the universal element. In the long run the universal element becomes subordinated and inevitably styleless style—that is, pure manner, merely native, untaught, uninspired, destitute of any not-ourselves ideal—usurps its place. This, in fact, is what to-day has largely taken place.

One reason for it, singularly enough, is the widespread popularity enjoyed by an incidental remark of Buffon himself. His "style is the man" has made the tour of the world and altogether eclipsed his forgotten definition. Epigrams sometimes turn out thankless children, and Buffon would have thought this one sharper than a serpent's tooth. It was pure *fioritura*. The famous "Discourse" as at first written did not contain it. It is an instance of the literary infirmity of adding a sententious truism, here ambiguous as well as superfluous, to an already adequately presented thesis. The result in this instance has been not a little ironical. The misconception of Buffon's idea is so easy, the correct interpretation so hard to state precisely enough to exclude the false; the context—which no one knows—is so necessary to elucidate the aphorism which itself is familiar to everyone. He is speaking of the learning, the data and discoveries (*faits et découvertes*) of a work—apparently having in mind a scientific work; "these things," he interjects, "are outside of a man," whereas the way in which they are arranged and presented is, of course, personal to the author. The style of the book, as distinct from the substance, is his. He doesn't mean that the writer's personal temperament leaves a deep impression on his style. "This is true," says one of his editors, M. Nollet, "but it is not Buffon's thought. He meant that the substance of a work, facts and discoveries, is common property, but that the style, that is the order and movement which one puts into his thoughts, belongs to the author alone, is his personal property." That is obviously not an observation about style in general, since it is strictly confined to *a* style in particular. It does not assert that there is no such thing as style in general. It does not maintain that the style is the writer's personal expression—merely that it is within his personal control in a sense in which data and discoveries are not. The style Buffon is speaking of, moreover, is the style of the book, not the author's style in general, not his characteristic manner if he have one, instinctive and particular. Quite independently of the writer's temperament he goes on, in true eighteenth-century fashion, to prescribe the different kinds of style appropriate to different kinds of topics. If the French language has any ambiguity it resides, one is sometimes tempted to think, in the different uses of the definite article, where correct interpretation sometimes depends on the context, sometimes eludes the elect—as is fair to conclude from its having in fact done so here. *Le style* here does not mean style in general any more than it means *the* characteristic style of the author. It means merely the style of the book in question, of a book, of any book. The sentence glossed by the context is as far as possible from meaning that style is nothing more than the idiosyncrasy of the writer manifested in his writing.

Architecture furnishes an illuminating if approximate illustration of the two different uses of the word style. There is a not too fanciful analogy between its different "styles" and the personal manner of the individual artist in all the arts. The several styles express each the temperament of its time as the artist's manner does his own. Yet they would certainly never have risen into existence as styles, would never have achieved their own centrality and coherence if they had not been inspired, each individual style in its own degree, with that spirit of style conceived as a universal æsthetic element which, besides crystallizing each into its own unity, makes it architecture as well as a style. Indeed it is the weakness of Renaissance as architecture, for example, that saps its strength as a style; just as the absence of style leaves the individual artist's manner structureless and as an instrument uncertain. Nothing could be more diverse to the eye than Greek and Gothic. The simplicity of one seems almost cellular, the complexity of the other, elaborately organic as far as the eye can trace the detail of the structure. Yet remark on the one hand the mere nomenclature of the trabeated style which is so elaborate as of itself to disclose the Greek simplicity as simplification, and, on the other, the fundamental interplay of majestic forces that constitutes the beauty as well as the grandeur of the loveliest as well as the most monumental Gothic. The difference between the two styles could not be greater, but it is not more marked than the identical element of style in both. As an individual artist conceives and executes his work in his own manner, each of them reflects the taste, the tone, the ideals, the character of its own age and clime, but like the individual artist whose work as well as being personal is marked by the impersonal quality of style, both Greek and Gothic architecture do more than merely embody the characteristic manner of thought and feeling of their respective periods and countries—one of philosophic calm, the other of energetic aspiration. In addition, both are interpenetrated with the spirit of order and movement, of abstract form vivifying concrete expression by pouring into it the universal elements of harmony and rhythm and thus not alone rendering the Parthenon and Amiens—say—vibrant with the mutual relations of their structural parts, but carrying into the conformation of all these details some subtly formative sense of the whole which they compose and by which in turn they, themselves, are consecrated with the chrism of style.

It would have much chagrined such a precisian as Buffon to have his incidental remark about a man's style being his own in contradistinction to the material that he shares with others, taken for a definition of style. He could hardly have comprehended such placid ignoring of the fact that he had already given and was expounding an altogether different theory and one quite insusceptible of being regarded as sanction for a go-as-you-please theory of literary composition—obviously ridiculous in any one of the rest of the seven arts. To have declared that a writer should put himself rather than order and movement into his thoughts would have been to cancel the "Discourse." On the other hand, a writer's manner, the personal strain in his style, is so important that, dealing with it at all, to have dealt with it only in an incidental interpolation would have been practically as absurd as to assert that a writer has only to express himself naturally to do so with style. He may have a natural aptitude for expressing himself with style. But this will be a natural aptitude for order and movement and not an aptitude for being natural. Buffon and his century before him dealt little with natural aptitudes and presupposed intelligence as evolution has since presupposed protoplasm. Even Rousseauism and the gospel of human perfectibility contemplated man's nature as plastic rather than as pre-established. The self-contradiction involved in associating nature, in which intention is absent, and art, in which it is vital, so closely as to deem their essence identical is one of the paradoxes of more recent times. The quality of naturalness indeed often shows as few traces of personality as of style. Since, for example, some of the wildest idiosyncrasies, so called, have been disclosed as due to "group consciousness"—not to say "mob psychology"—it has been more difficult to revere eccentricity as self-expression. The traits of a personality saturated with the mimetic may be better sought in the model than in the mimic. They lose their tang in transmission. The naturalness of the parrot and the mocking-bird is personality at one remove, and what Echo sighs to us from some distant isle is, alas! what we have already heard.

Personality is minimized thus in naturalness of a certain order—the naturalness of a natural born natural, for example; it needs acquisitions of its own to round out instinct into character. Of course, there are other varieties. Mr. H. M. Tomlinson, of the London *Nation* and the author of charming books, was recently quoted as asserting in dogmatic, in fact in Dogberry, vein that "a literary style is not as some fond critics imagine a deliberately acquired vice. A man just has it. When he is really a writer he does not know he has any style. He has something to say; and he says it in the only way that comes easy to him"—regardless of the hard reading thus made according to Sheridan's sadly true observation. "Only those writers are concerned about their style," he sternly adds, "who should be employed at something more useful." Mr. Tomlinson is "really a writer," and perhaps he "just has" his gift of style. But apparently he just doesn't have it always. Very likely he has it oftener when he has something to tell than when he has, as here, something to say; the two *genres* differ in difficulty. And he is so delightful when he does have it that from our point of view he could hardly be employed at anything more useful than in being concerned about it. Why in any case should he discourage others? If style be a vice, how should it be the only one that can't be acquired?

As to a man's not knowing he has any style when he does have it, we should hardly know what Mr. Tomlinson means if in so many quarters just now there were not observable such a light-hearted zest in playing the game of existence blindfold—consciousness, formerly defined as "the light of all our seeing," having fallen into much disrepute if not "every day in every way" still often and variously. Only blindly, one would say, can many of the self-styled temperamental players develop the confidence needed to sustain a morale to which mere presumption must prove a broken reed. The mood of the moment, perhaps more exactly than the spirit of the times, is so adventurous and irresponsible as to have given the abhorred name of "repression" to the old "arch-enemy of mankind" and exalted the subliminal self to the position of guardian angel. Accordingly philosophy of the unconscious now under such full sail seems also bound for such ports as may be discovered under a roving commission. Mr. Santayana is perhaps the last philosopher whom one should expect to remind us of Scott's remark to Lockhart: "I fear you have some very young ideas in your head." Yet where either art or woman is concerned, who would forego the advantages of young ideas? His declaration "Art is like a charming woman who once had her age of innocence in the nursery when she was beautiful without knowing it, being wholly intent on what she was making or telling or imagining" sounds less like a master than like a bachelor of arts—at any rate, the arts of design, whether plastic or feminine. The precautionary words "nursery" and "when she was beautiful without knowing it" naturally imply an infancy fairly inarticulate, but one imagines that in either case articulate adolescence has more than a vague notion of what it is about, and that process as well as substance shared the intention of early art as well as of the youthful artist to whom Mr. Santayana refers. Consciousness of how and whether they were succeeding, and obvious inferences therefrom, must have attended effort where attainment is predicated on aim; and subsequent progress, at all events, could hardly have proceeded from aimless groping. The untrained and up-to-date boy who, occupied in drawing on his slate a figure which he said represented God, replied to an objection that no one knew how He looked, "Well, they will when I get this done," demanded too much credulity. The pleistocene mammoth outline is more authentic and doubtless more admirable, and, particularly, more skillful than uninstructed improvisation. To argue from Fra Angelico's apparent naïveté, seen from our angle, either his own ingenuousness or that of his age, is no sounder than ascribing affectation to Puvis de Chavannes, who plaintively remarked when charged with imitating the Primitives: "Why not say I have the same temperament?" Even less sound, since one might, in view of the difference between the "Primitive" times and our own, reply to Puvis with some degree of plausibility, "Because you couldn't have. Too much has happened since." In any case in all art early or late the element of style is of too universal substance and application to be identified with the individuality of whose intelligent expression it is clearly and consciously, even when instinctively, an instrument—when indeed it is not, as in some instances seemingly it is, an end in itself. And it had certainly much better be an end in itself, subordinating all personality and achieving at least an ordered and rhythmic result, than illustrate the kind of feeling and functioning to be associated in many instances with unconsciousness.

Personality in a work of art being, as has been aptly observed, not what you put in but what you can't leave out, style may, precisely, be taken as what on the other hand (as Buffon asserted) you put in. But necessarily what you can't leave out colors to a certain or rather an uncertain extent what you put in, and accordingly personality shows in, but is not, your style—any more than your clothes which you select are how you wear them. No more capital example of the distinction between manner and style need be sought than that furnished by the writings of Carlyle, rich in both elements. Everything is energy in Carlyle. Energy is as apparent in the restraint of the elegy on Edward Irving as in the extravagance of "Shooting Niagara." And energy implies emphasis and underlines whatever it expresses. Hence we can more distinctly in Carlyle's case than in most others recognize the several expressions of his genius, that is to say, his energy; genius, being, as Arnold says, "mainly an affair of energy." Again, we can more easily discriminate his manner from his style not only because both have so much relief but because we can catch his manner almost in the act of invading his style. Partly this was chronological, in other words exhibited a tendency that grew upon him. But partly also it was an infiltration of his conscious art by his personal whim, owing to the release of the latter by raising the flood-gates of his restraint as he conceived occasion to call for it; the style of the "Sterling," for example, is simple, tranquil, and altogether on a more elevated plane than that of the earlier "Sartor." At the same time Fitzjames Stephen would not have chosen a passage from it as he did from "Sartor" to set against a passage from Mill illustrating, as he said, the genius of the greatest poet of his age contrasted with that of the greatest logician. And I think myself that perhaps we could better dispense with those works of Carlyle in which style predominates than those which his personality saturates. Still one gets a little tired of this latter, and it was doubtless thinking of it that led Mr. W. B. Yeats to speak of someone's "harsh voice" giving, in reading it aloud, "almost a quality of style to Carlylean commonplace." There is nothing restful in tireless tumultuousness. The victim's personality wearies the reader. One would prefer a victor—self-control as spectacle always outshining the lack of it; except with the "ecstasists."

Thackeray's exclamation, after a generous tribute to Carlyle's personal dignity, "I wish he would hang up his d—d old fiddle," is a comprehensible cry of protest against too much personal expression. Taine's preference of "Esmond" over and almost to the exclusion of the rest of his work witnesses the same weariness in Thackeray's own case. In the case of genius—not common enough to make it imperative to do so!—one can hardly decide. Here one hesitates to exalt style at the expense of manner, and may settle the difficulty by breathing a wish that the manner of both Thackeray on occasion and Carlyle often had been less mannered. Personality is the irreducible element in the incomprehensible phenomenon of genius. Thackeray and Carlyle are, for us at any rate, of even greater interest than their style, than their art. At least Thackeray's style and art owe a large part of their charm to his own extraordinary personal appeal. But the vast field of literary and æsthetic interest rewards consideration of the rule rather than of the exception among its figures and their functioning, when we are dealing with principles, even though Kant's "universal norm" may here be unattainable. There is also this to be observed of the personality of genius: that its superior interest, its signal fascinations, being less comprehensible in all their fulness to other generations than they are to their own, must inevitably merge with their contemporaries of lesser eminence as both recede into the past, aside from the new competitions they must sustain when Bacon's "next ages" with a different succession of cloud-capped peaks and sunlit summits come into view. Then, indeed, manner may congratulate itself on having, at whatever sacrifice, clothed itself in style. Style will commend it to the posterity that its manner may conceivably confuse and chill. Its style will be the language of posterity also, however different its taste, its fashions. It was really Thackeray's manner, not his style, that Mr. Max Beerbohm meant when he said it was "getting a little eighteen-sixty." Of his style the "perfection" of which Carlyle called unrivalled "in our day," Mr. Beerbohm says in exquisite style of his own: "He blew on his pipe and words came tripping around him, like children, like pretty little children who are perfectly drilled for the dance; or came, did he will it, treading in their precedence, like kings, gloomily." Order and movement could not be more specifically signalized—or exemplified.

On the other hand, when Thackeray remarked, "I may quarrel with Mr. Dickens's art a thousand and a thousand times; I delight and wonder at his genius," he undoubtedly meant in large part that Dickens's art was disfigured by mannerisms, that his manner, in other words, dominated and distorted his style, of which facetiousness is as characteristic as caricature is of his characters. Both these defects of his qualities of vitality and imagination have been obstacles to Dickens's attaining rank as an artist commensurate with his fairly wonderful genius, and it is only since art has suffered its present eclipse in the shadow of genius, real or imagined, that lovers of paradox like Mr. Chesterton and detached temperaments like Mr. Santayana have found it piquant to minimize or ignore—or vaunt—them. Also the current revival of interest in Dickens shown by our younger writers may be due, as well as to the attraction of novelty inherent in rehabilitations, to a fellow-feeling on the part of our own facetiousness, which has been called the curse of the country. One may doubt nevertheless if he is read as much as he is lauded. Temperamental similarity may warm in idea to what would bore it in fact—one of those phenomena which Carlyle, when too full for utterance, used to call "significant of much." Our time and our country, especially since our social development has reached its present flourishing phase, seem peculiarly sensitive to the satisfactions, than which we certainly find few more intimate, of what is, too brutally, known as "raising a laugh." The English, who savor these satisfactions less, we accuse, not altogether humorously, of lacking either humor or the sense of it. We have a slight feeling as if of injury at their refusal, or estrangement at what we fancy their inability, to play with us. Dickens, however, ought to be a bond between us. The facetiousness which, whether for good or ill, is one of our national traits and which, as one may say, has infiltrated our national style, certainly dictated the order and movement which he put into his thoughts to an extent that makes his manner so markedly mannerism as practically to identify it with his style. The ideal in his case would be the converse procedure—style invading manner so as to minimize mannerism.

Absolutely to proscribe mannerism would surely savor of pedantry. In the hands or rather in the fibre of an instinctive artist it is sometimes just the element needed to set the final touch on manner itself, to add the flavor to the confection, to endue the manner that expresses the artist's individuality with the personal reminder of intimacy which endears—unless, as of course it may, it estranges. An instance is that which makes one of the most delightful traits of one of the most delightful of our actresses undervalued by routine proscription of mannerism that is piquant along with that which is flat. If nothing is so flat as excess, on the other hand nothing is so engaging as quality in fragrance that is faint but distinct. It is only of what is too little that we say we cannot have too much. Dickens gave us a surfeit of facetiousness. He was so much an actor—not being one—as to suffer his manner, become mannerism, to histrionize his style, the conscious field of his art, by which he set great store, but which he so personalized with the manner of which he was still fonder as to rob it of the objective quality that, precisely, makes art of expression. He conceived his manner as style. He has passage after passage in what one might call the voluntarily stylistic vein that probably irritated Thackeray much more than Bulwer's "height of fine language" did Yellowplush. But taken at the flood, even these passages, perhaps they especially, were apt to turn into the channel of facetiousness where the temptation to be funny becomes irresistible. Thereupon verbiage *sostenuto*, as in Mark Twain the idea *da capo*. If Mark Twain, however, had thought he was being "stylistic" in the process he would probably not have got the laugh that he rarely failed finally to get and that, I should suppose, Dickens gets now mainly through his matter.

Mark Twain's method was sapiently direct. Yet the best, in the sense of the starkest, example of it that I remember was furnished by one of our "minstrels," in days when our humor of a certain grade was masked by burnt cork, when our humorous entertainments were explicit and professional, and not yet amateur and postprandial. This artist came to the front of the stage and in a sulky, then a shamefaced, then a resigned, and finally a savage manner remarked many times in an appalling crescendo ending in a shouting climax that his girl lived in Yonkers. The public, at first uninterested, finally capitulated in convulsions of glee. The same effect I recall obtained by Mark Twain at a dinner given to Mr. Brander Matthews—by his friends, and thus a large though an intimate occasion. In richly varied framework Clemens used essentially the same means of repeating antiphonally, in various tones ranging from the sepulchral to the ferocious, but all weirdly drawling, what he pretended (with obviously no warrant of either truth or caricature, to constitute either wit or humor) was the singularly sinister name of the evening's guest. I remember no occasion of more prolonged and luxurious mirth than each of these. Meanwhile, naturally, the responsible faculties were more or less in abeyance. They will not however stay there and, the glamour of the occasion vanished, we feel that this sort of thing, well worthy of being called genius (if that does it any real good), can't be kept up. The dosage can't be increased—a necessity for conserving its effect. Nor can one's appreciation of it be communicated to benighted consumers of a different brand of stimulant. For this there is too much personality and too little style about it. To secure permanence in the æsthetic product the preservative quality of the latter element is needed. Without it, art is as fleeting as fashion; which is no more than saying that language has a greater chance of survival than jargon. None the less, it cannot be gainsaid that personality is the most interesting thing in the world, and the proper study of mankind. Personality, therefore, expressing itself in style, achieves at once the most interesting and the most lasting æsthetic result.

It is, however, essential to remember that personality is an exceedingly complicated affair. Undoubtedly what in any work of art captivates or alienates, interests or wearies the critical spirit, the connoisseur, or even the amateur, is, as Sainte-Beuve testified of himself, the mind of the artist—meaning by mind, of course, both intellect and feeling. Yes, and, considered as a cause, will also. Is the artist's mind in any given case crude or cultivated, is it common or distinguished, listless or energetic? What are its endowments and acquisitions, its capacity and equipment, aside from the machinery concerned with the immediate matter in hand? And, fundamentally, abstract qualities as informing the concrete work are what we note; taken together they are *its* style—that is to say, its manner plus style, if it have style. But if it be a work of any æsthetic value, little reflection is needed to assure us that the faculty behind it is something considerably more complicated than a "gift" that the artist "just had." Even if he originally had it in germ he didn't have it in its maturity or "just" have it in his own. From the standpoint of style the infant phenomenon that does not develop is apt to remain permanently promising—a condition well known as calculated to make the heart sick. Blind Tom remains less interesting than Paderewsky. Paderewsky himself is chained to the keyboard. The Morphys of chess keep in form and study new problems, I believe. And the Hoppes of billiards and Ty Cobbs of baseball were not altogether born so.

A predisposition for style is no doubt as much as a predisposition for anything else a natural gift. Of what is natural and what is acquired there are, in general, no statistics. What we can safely say is that neither is apt to flourish in isolation; the Pitcairn Islanders produced little of either of any recorded value. But style itself is not to be confounded with a predisposition for it—any more than dancing. It is not a natural gift like manner. The part that consciousness plays in it is far greater. Compared with it, manner is, if not wholly instinctive, at least largely a subconscious acquisition. Presumably even negro sculpture first learned what it teaches its votaries in "modern art." Up to a certain point, at least, learning how means learning someone else's how. Such instances as Maupassant's seven years of application under the austere tutelage of Flaubert with nothing to show for it—save a miraculous style!—and Stevenson's long apprenticeship as the sedulous ape indicate the effect of study and practice. They may be set against such pronouncements as that of Mr. Tomlinson. To his: "Only those writers are concerned about their style who should be employed at something more useful," one is tempted to reply in the same cavalier terms: those writers who are *not* concerned about their style could be employed at nothing else *as* useful. "Both" may very well be the answer to the question whether the style of a writer distinguished for his style is natural or acquired; as Mill settled the classics-*vs.*-mathematics controversy of his day by asking if the tailor should make coats or trousers. Meantime Lessing's preference of the pursuit to the possession of truth formulates a genuine instinct and has a universal appeal. It is justified even in the most august of instances. Job's inquiry: "Canst thou by searching find out God?" does not impeach Isaiah's injunction: "Seek ye the Lord while he may be found."

Any persistent analysis runs up every æsthetic enigma in the end to its basis in talent, and talent is the incalculable factor in the artistic equation. At the same time its functioning, which *can* be analyzed, furnishes synthesis with the most trustworthy basis for constructive formulations. Miss Rebecca West, who says that "a school-girl today knows more of the mechanics of writing than great artists knew half a century ago," refers of course to English school-girls. Our own would, perhaps, claim less, some of them undoubtedly being quite aware how deeply the mechanics of current writing are indebted to the great artists from whose practice their principles are so largely generalized. In any case the Cimmerian stretches unilluminated by talent, however populous with mechanically equipped school-girls, the critic may profitably consider too speculative a field for his exploring—a field wherein, as Carlyle observed of Coleridge's excursions, it would be "uncertain what game you would catch or whether any." I remember Rodin once dismissing some such speculation as irrelevant by saying, "That would only be true of a mediocre artist." When Lemaitre urges a spirit of sympathy only in approaching those of our contemporaries who reward criticism, he is more convincing than when he himself adopts a spirit of antipathy in considering—instead of a literary topic, he incidentally remarked—the work of Georges Ohnet. Style without talent, in a word, need not detain one long. And a talent for it of course stamps a style in its own image and superscription. But this is not saying that a talent for it is the same thing as talent in general. Talent, therefore, we need not attempt to define in considering, at least in its general features, an element that so markedly differentiates it. Individuality may, and often does, express itself as visibly in style as in any other form of expression, but this no more makes of style itself an individual matter than changing a dollar affects its value. The reality of goodness itself is not disproved by such differing types as Peter and John exhibiting different orders of sainthood. Speaking of one style as good and of another as bad presupposes a single element good in one case and bad in another. To say that an element is only found in combination is not to deny its existence. The abstract is as actual as the concrete —life, as real as the agencies it animates. Individual talent, therefore, which eludes analysis, does not in stamping its image on style, endue with its own elusiveness the element of style itself. One would hardly think of thus elaborating the point if defining style as the man were not a highly speculative bit of simplification which has missed a cog; or if every now and then someone with authority, as for instance, I suppose, the editor of the London *Adelphi*, who has written a book about style concluding "there are styles but no style," did not similarly belittle it. It has been remarked of Lewes's "Biographical History of Philosophy" that it had obviously been written to show there was no such thing as its subject. Philosophy can very well take care of itself—sure of survival in philosophizing in any case; but practically, I think style suffers from the disposition to ignore it as an element with qualities of its own and consider it merely as a resultant of the intricate forces resident in the inexplicable individuality of a personal talent.

To call anything the natural expression of a personal talent is certainly not to say very much about it and does not get us very far. It does not even distinguish it from other natural expressions of the same talent. The word "natural" is also ambiguous. According to Professor Josey of Dartmouth College, who has written a suggestive analysis of instinct from the standpoint of society rather than that of psychology alone, the quality of "naturalness" shows far fewer traces of personality than it used to be credited with before, sociologically examined, its essentially parasitic origin appeared as pure responsiveness to purely external stimuli. To learn that "self-expression" and "living one's own life" are thus, scientifically analyzed, merely reactions of crude passivity to the earliest and most elementary of external influences, instead of the satisfaction of divine personal impulses breaking the bonds of artificial "suppression," should arouse distrust in the authority and minimize the categorical imperative of these watchwords of verdancy. It is sad to reflect but apparently true that in much "self-expression" we get but faint traces of personality of any pungency, and that in "living one's own life" in defiance of "the devil" of discipline, one risks being swept along with the highly homogeneous horde of depressingly undifferentiated individuals bound helter-skelter for the precipitous shores of "the deep sea."

There is, however, a consideration that if observed should tend to circumvent so promiscuous a fate as this last. It is not technical and can hardly be formularized. But, though of a general nature, it has, in current phraseology, a certain inspirational value—implying a kind of literary and artistic regeneration through the agency of the regent of our faculties, that centre from which these radiate and to which they return. Besides instinct and mind, in short, there is in personality another factor that has a bearing on style too important to overlook. Spenser suggests it in two lines of the "Hymne in Honoure of Beautie."

> "For of the soul the bodie form doth take:
> For soule is form and doth the body make."

And for this factor, Goethe, perhaps the most explicit exemplar as well as advocate of development of quality through culture, evidently thought cultivation could do a good deal. "Altogether, the style of a writer," he observed to Eckermann, obviously agreeing more nearly with Spenser than with Mr. Tomlinson, "is a faithful representative of his mind; therefore . . . if any would write in a noble style, let him first possess a noble soul." He himself was neither content with what he "just had," to begin with, nor discouraged by thinking he just had to put up with it. Far from believing he could be "employed at something more useful," and unaware of any quixotism in the attempt, he proceeds: "As I am a human being and as such have human faults and weaknesses, my writings cannot be free from them. Yet as I was constantly bent on my improvement and always striving to ennoble myself I was in a state of constant progress." "Human faults and weaknesses," "bent on my improvement," "striving to ennoble myself," "a state of constant progress," how quaintly these phrases fall on the ear today! How unlike "living one's own life" and "expressing one's own personality"—the kind, too, that one "just has." But on the other hand how cheerful they sound beside Mr. Tomlinson, how modest, in spite of being in a state of constant progress, beside those who revere impulse as sacrosanct and acclaim instinct as a guiding-star.

And how did the veteran of seventy-five maintain and, so to say, consolidate his position? "Today after dinner," says Eckermann, "Goethe went through a portfolio containing some works of Raphael in order to keep up a constant intercourse with that which is best and to accustom himself to muse upon the thoughts of a great man." Hence, perhaps, in some degree and undoubtedly from general culture as well as specific study, the difference between the violence of "Goetz" at the beginning of his career and the beautiful benignity of the "Faust" dedication at its culmination. In spite of a remarkable memory, Eckermann probably failed to get everything just right. It is more likely that Goethe mused upon his own thoughts stimulated by the style of Raphael, whose genius for expression in that universal language if ever elsewhere equalled was at all events the main thing about him, and one than which no example can be found of a greater natural gift more supremely developed. If Raphael had gone on reflecting Perugino and Goethe had multiplied "Goetzes"—as, but for the culture that develops seed into fruit of substance and flower of form, fertilizing and pruning manner into style, they conceivably might have done—the course of art and letters would, in considerable measure, it is probable, have lacked an element, both exemplary and constructive, which has in no slight degree contributed to elevation of thought, nobility of feeling, and sensitiveness to beauty throughout the western world.

But to this order and movement with which the spirit of style endows the expression of beauty there has probably never—until our own day—been any general blindness except in the ages that were blind to art itself. Outside of these centuries of darkness in western Europe, the artist, who from Egypt down has consciously conceived and skillfully executed embodiments of it without number and beyond praise, has certainly never closed his eyes to it until the present century. Nor has that province and rank of literature in virtue of which Carlyle calls it "the Thought of Thinking Souls," and which among other things has either illustrated or illuminated those æsthetic principles that bridge the interval between the artist and his public. In fact, Bacon did not wait for Buffon's definition thus to describe, any more than to exemplify, style, and substantially so describes it himself. In "Of Beauty" he says, "that of favour [features] is more than that of colour; and that of decent and gracious motion more than that of favour." And, "A man shall see faces that if you examine them part by part you shall find never a good, and yet all together do well"; and again, "the principal part of Beauty is in decent motion." There one has organic order and ordered movement given as composing the chief element of beauty. Bacon had only to bracket them with the vinculum "style"—a matter of terminology—to anticipate Buffon. It is significant that nowhere else in the "Essays" does he treat of style, or indeed use the word—save once in the sense of "title." He thought ill of the individual manner of the painter who disregarded the cardinal points he mentions: "A man cannot tell whether Apelles or Albert Dürer were the more trifler: whereof the one would make a personage by geometrical proportions"—substituting mere statement for rhythm—"the other by taking the parts out of divers faces to make one excellent"—involving the loss of organic quality, since—"a painter may make a better face than ever was," but "must do it by a kind of felicity (as a musician that maketh an excellent air in music)." This felicity has, perhaps, been usually taken as in agreement with the inspirational theory of style, but I imagine that Bacon did not consider the making of an excellent air in music altogether automatic and he evidently considered his painter's feat exceptional. In disapproving artifice and routine, he does not imply that nature's suggestiveness can be felicitously exploited by an unaided natural gift. He believed too thoroughly in his own empirical method. He would have argued: the more expertness the greater felicity, the greater experience the more expertness. It is indeed for this reason that the indirect bearing on style and manner in his writing directly of beauty has its interest. He has, besides, a notable sense for style, a kind of unfailing *flair* for it, and, so to say, follows its scent even when uninspired by its spirit. But though he seldom soars, he does not stray.

Direct testimony from the stately Gibbon is also thoroughly interesting as based on practical mastery as well as on perception. "The style of an author should be the image of his mind," he says, "but the choice and command of language is the fruit of exercise." He emphasizes thus the important part played by personality in a man's style and reprehends its denaturing, but in the choice and command of language, obviously a phrase for the element of style in general, he insists on the necessity of repeated effort; and it is in virtue of this "effort" that his own first volume in distinction from its successors—also written by Buffon's "*l'homme même*"—earned from Horace Walpole the apt epithet "enamelled." His remark may be expanded into counsel that an author's manner, which, according to Sainte-Beuve, proceeds from the nature of his talent and which is what clings to and colors his expression in spite of himself, thus imaging his mind in fact, should not be so allowed to lose its character in its fusion with the order and movement that are the fruit of exercise and taking thought, as to misinterpret his personality and miss therefore, in the case of a personality of interest, what Bacon calls "a kind of felicity" securing an effect of beauty. The particular, in a word, in assuming the general, individual thought in informing and modelling language or any other order of plastic statement, is to avoid distortion though submitting to discipline.

These are the true terms on which style that is neither solely style nor solely manner is to be realized. The modification of natural manner may in given cases be very slight, and style be assimilated by manner through mere affinity, but style is—in *its* nature—too markedly general and objective, too integrally treatment rather than theme, to be otherwise than consciously acquired. It does not present a formula to be followed, for it has none, but it exacts the coöperation of attentive apprenticeship. However predisposed by predilection and endowments the practitioner may be, he will hardly endue a particular design of any dignity or intricacy with corresponding universal qualities unless through discipline he has developed his personality, or has acquired more of his art than can be either divined or merely taken for granted. At any rate, the quality of style, that is, of an *ensemble* of structure and rhythm, paralleling, as it were, in the treatment the purely intellectual extension of its theme—else a series of statements—he will miss, in its ideal fulness and richness, if his equipment is restricted to his native aptitudes. Aptitudes, to be sure, do not exclude advancement, and few talents nowadays would need to luxuriate in undirected and undisciplined functioning if they did not—as so many do—determinedly prefer doing so. The machinery of education is so vast, so multifarious, so apparently inescapable—and so important also in the discovery, without speaking of the development, of a "natural gift"—that it may fairly be considered as the environment from which such "natural gift" itself is unconsciously absorbed. And certainly for the acquisition and maturing of those elements of art that are consciously acquired and slowly matured—including style first of all, in all but extremely exceptional cases—education is as indispensable as it is effective and benign.

III

THE ART OF PROSE

WITH the forces at command of which I have spoken—with attentive regard for order and movement and, under their influence, utilization of the abounding, if a little bit monotonous, manner and personality today vouchsafed to us—is it quixotism to cherish, among other æsthetic visions, the ideal of a richer prose than that which is today our ideal, the ideal in a word of æsthetic rather than of purely communicative prose? Logically the thread I have been following would lead to such an ideal—one that should fuse style and manner, on terms implying both the disciplinary and the inspiring influence upon manner of the spirit of order and movement, and the endowment in turn of this spirit, which is of universal application, with the particular and personal character that, in a talent of any value, inevitably stamps and colors the concrete result. Only by this welding of what he can't keep out with what consciously—even if, in fortunate cases, easily—he puts in, is the artist likely to achieve in anything like completeness the artistic potentialities of whatever problem he is attacking, of whatever conception he is endeavoring to realize or of whatever subject he wishes to present, to develop, to communicate.

Naturally, what consciously he puts in is what costs him his effort and monopolizes his mind. *Hic labor, hoc opus, est.* Hence possibly the decline of style in a labor-saving age. Hence the rarity of that "power and skill with which the evolution of his poems is conducted" ascribed by Arnold to Gray, and of the pleasure we get when at any point we feel what Mr. Sherman has called "the formative pressure of the tone and structure of the entire work." This last remark, indeed, may be deemed quite the formula for the view here taken—the "tone" being, let us say, altogether native and, if one chooses, originally instinctive, but consciously utilized together with the conscious "structure" as "formative pressure" throughout the work as a whole, and in that way inducing the sense and illustrating the spirit of style. At any rate the cultivation of the conscious field—the only one that *can* be cultivated—though laborious, has hitherto been found profitable by civilization.

There is, however, another strain in the temper of the age hostile to the genius of style besides that egotism and its derivative laziness which Spinoza deplored, I believe, above other human weaknesses.

These latter traits are general and are vaunted rather than dissembled by those who illustrate them, to whom they wear the aspect of self-respect and inspiration. It is hardly unparliamentary, therefore, to refer to them as general, if we bear in mind that the current egotism or self-respect does not exclude respect for others (if like-minded) nor the prevailing inspirational indolence conflict with the dominant industrial note that hums so steadily in various sections of the contemporary æsthetic domain. But these are practical forces, in full and largely automatic activity, and, at least so far as literary expression in English prose is concerned, style has of late years suffered, I think, quite as sensibly, if not as much, from a definite theory that it is constituted by certain elements that in reality only condition it.

Prose of course is vastly our most general as well as most copious medium of articulate expression and in spite of the flood of verse, bond and free, is what for the most part is understood in current discussion of the subject of style; it would be exact, I imagine, to say that though style is considered when poetry is discussed, when style is discussed prose is intended. The elements I refer to are simplicity and clarity—or, shaded a trifle, directness and precision. How much better, how extraordinarily much better, it would be to concentrate these admirable qualities in the domain of thought rather than upon expression. The gain from such a transfer appears—in theory anyhow—the more you reflect upon it the more worth while. Then if your purely clear and simple style did not take care of itself, automatically following significance clear and simple, you could arrange for its doing so in the collegiate rather than in the post-graduate curriculum. The latter might preferably preoccupy itself with the æsthetic values of the subject.

In so doing it could hardly fail to realize the limitations of our prose ideal of simplicity and clarity and the advantage of enduing these qualities, even in instances where their heightening by emotional color is not called for, with the order and movement of style. That simplicity and clarity once attained will of themselves disclose this order and movement is a superstition, born perhaps of the difficulty of attaining them—a difficulty great enough no doubt to have its surmounting thus crowned if such things were arranged on the reward of merit principle. They are, however, arranged differently, and further effort is necessary even after thought is clarified before its expression becomes style, though I am proceeding on the presumption that we might not too tragically tax our indolence if we elevated our prose ideal enough to stimulate this broader and more exacting practice. No doubt we should have to try in order to find out about that. I think the experiment in any case would be an interesting one, and even if any elevation of our present ideal proved to involve considerably increased mental activity, that result might easily be worth what it might cost. Certainly when the heightening of emotional color *is* called for, when we feel stirred and wish to communicate the feeling, we might find that we succeeded better, even if we had to take greater pains, by confining ourselves less rigidly merely to stating the fact—if, in a word, we invoked the genius of order and movement instead of the spirit of statistics. And undoubtedly we should find succeeding better agreeable.

Attic prose is assuredly admirable and Asiatic often meretricious, but it is quite possible to avoid the latter without attaining the former. The injunction "Cease to do evil" demands its sequel, "Learn to do good." Otherwise lethargy ensues. And—at least so far as classification is concerned! —why should not our prose be some third kind, neither Asiatic nor yet Attic, but an eclectic with the virtues of both and the faults or failures of neither; or rather a development of our own needs and nature, guided by what these have to suggest to us. In the field of the imagination we have amassed so much treasure of remembered experience, notably emotional, which the antique world did not possess, as to make exclusively rational concentration seem of necessity limited as a comprehensive ideal, however much—however grossly in fact—we may need it as an element in both thought and style. Lincoln's Gettysburg addresss suits us better than Pericles's funeral oration, so much has happened between their respective eras—Christianity for one thing, romanticism for another. And there is nothing in realism really to warrant an arid style.

To be driven by Burke's excesses to exaltation of Addison's sedateness betrays too clearly the didactic strain in Arnold's criticism. Not that there can be any objection made, especially in criticism, to desiring "that the good may prevail," which phrase from the "Agamemnon" he cites as the aspiration of all the higher literature since, as indeed it must still be unless one views the human scene with the dreamy eye of the ruminants of the field. If this animal attitude toward the function of literature were not so popular just now it would seem extraordinary—instead of wearisome—that holding it should be congruous with the possession of an emotional organization sufficiently sensitive at all to expand and contract in sympathy with the subject it studies, the thesis it expounds. And one need not be a thorough believer in the current doctrine of "Hands off! Let 'em have a good time," or a devotee of the art for art gospel, and may even take a human interest in human welfare, and still hold that literature and art are not really to be evaluated with sole reference to their exemplary reproduction in an indefinite future. So regarding them the eye of criticism is on the wrong object. For criticism the parent has a prior claim over the progeny. The latter might perhaps advantageously be left to the consideration of instructors of youth who no doubt best know how to serve their interests and secure their well-being. To instil—or, more deferentially speaking, to persuade—is to criticism more pertinent than to instruct and, though more difficult, is also more decorous.

Arnold's preoccupation with education had every warrant, and its overflow into his criticism in the main the happiest result, but in this field it led him to develop a fondness for categories to which our indebtedness is great, but which was not always quite consonant with his own critical genius. This fondness, joined with the fact that his æsthetic side was a shade academic, led him roundly to exile the æsthetic element from the domain of prose and bid it take refuge in that of poetry, where exclusively, he considered, it belonged. After quoting at length one of Ruskin's beautiful and moving passages, and praising it heartily, he adds: "All the critic could possibly suggest in the way of objection would be perhaps that Mr. Ruskin is there trying to make prose do more than it can perfectly do; that what he is there attempting he will never, except in poetry, be able to accomplish to his entire satisfaction." One may agree or not about Ruskin, but must reflect that there are practical difficulties in the way of turning so short a corner as that of a different art whenever a writer inclines to quicken his expression with emotion—as when, to borrow from the passage in question, looking up from Swiss lakes toward Alpine heights one beholds, in Ruskin's words, "the waves of everlasting green roll silently into their long inlets among the shadows of the pines." Considering the lack of solidity in much of his matter, and the submersion of form by color, the lack of serenity, in his style, Ruskin's prose no doubt often justifies speculation as to whether his position as a classic would not be more secure if, after receiving the Newdigate prize for poetry, he had continued to express himself in verse—that acknowledged antidote for his especial defect of emotional excess in expression. Even so he has given us a body of admirable æsthetic prose from which multitudes of readers have received pleasure justly to be called exquisite, as well as, it is true, no small amount of the "fine writing" which does tempt taste to think longingly by contrast of the elevated composure which is Attic alone. His prose nevertheless is full of rapturous cadences well worth the tension of alertness in picking one's way through morasses of the meretricious far more extensive than his.

Burke's taste is certainly Asiatic on occasion. Arnold adduces a succession of citations exhibiting his prose as "somewhat barbarously rich and overloaded." Apparently he would have preferred Burke to write the Attic prose of Addison to which he gives his highest praise, content to call its ideas negligible. But had Burke written the prose of Addison, would he have called him our greatest prose writer? I think not. Face to face with this central question he would have thrown over his "prose of the centre," or at least have been careful to distinguish it from distinctly prosaic prose. There is an element in poetry as in plastic art, for the absence of which, wherever it is apt, we must in sober truth, acknowledge that absolutely nothing can wholly compensate—the element of beauty, the æsthetic element. Why should prose be robbed of it? The fundamental weakness of prose poetry is not so much that the poetry is out of character as regards its mood as that it is out of place in its form of expression. Prose may be anything but lyric in order and movement. Wherever it is pertinent, beauty of any kind is priceless. To be cheated of it by categories would be inept.

It is, nevertheless, one of Arnold's signal services to his generation—and to subsequent ones—measurably to have distinguished for them the province at once and the nature of poetry on the one hand, and of prose on the other. Everyone interested in criticism will recall his exposition and the part played in it by what he called his "turn for the French." The French genius for prose, proceeding from the superiority of their intelligence to their genius and imagination—so that even in poetry it is their intelligence that is most marked and prose is their best, being their native, expression, as poetry is that of the English—clearly suggested, he maintained, that English prose had something to learn from French measure, restraint, clearness, and conformity to recognized standards of tone and taste. All this was so sound and at the time so impressive (being withal so unsuspected!) and has since become so thoroughly a part of our thinking and feeling upon this extremely central and consequently widely suggestive subject, that it has quite generally been accepted as final. There is certainly this to be said for Arnold's contention, that probably more than any other agency it is to be credited with having, in contemporary prose style, brought into disrepute the meretricious and the mediocre as these seductions solicit the cultivated writer. This is perhaps especially true among ourselves, our customary prose having, no doubt, lagged a little behind that of Britain in moderating the magniloquence of its pre-Victorian phases and being even in Arnold's day more in need of his austere counsels; though in even earlier days we were sometimes still farther behindhand in substance than in style. At Harvard, I believe, they were discussing whether or no Adam had an umbilical cord long after Oxford had given up the problem in despair. Yet, significant as Arnold's doctrine was, there is also this to be added about it, namely, that the qualities it assigns to the nature of prose, though characteristic, are not of necessity as exclusive, and that the limits it assigns to its practice are not of necessity as rigid, as his view implied. We fell in love with the disciplinary side of the doctrine and it is not to be denied that its inhibitions resulted automatically in stricter form as well as in purer taste, in positive values as well as in negative virtues.

But the categories "prose" and "verse" are too rigidly conceived when the æsthetic or emotional element of expression is strictly confined to one of them. Aside from the practical difficulties I speak of in possessing in its fulness—in any such fulness as Arnold did—the technic of both, the exclusion of this element from the realm of prose is too rigorous. Arnold's own prose practice is by no means always and everywhere consistent with this view. Nor was he unresponsive to the æsthetic note in the prose of others, from the Authorized Version to foreign languages. He has himself recorded being hypnotized to the point of "perpetually declaiming" some of the prose of Maurice de Guérin, the rhythm of which "had lodged itself" in his head. At that time obviously he was less didactic. But since no one who thinks at all systematically would, if possessed in any degree of the social instinct, do so solely to his own glory, and hope thereby wholly to escape the didactic contagion, I may acknowledge the conviction that it would be an excellent thing if we had more prose the rhythm of which lodged itself in one's head. The whole point is there.

Excluding prose from the realm preëmpted by formal poetry—where it is inevitably at a disadvantage and where by definition it has no business, having its own character, which it compromises in leaving its own province—by no means involves its exclusion from the far larger domain of art, where if it have style it belongs. Without style it becomes what, in 1868, Scherer complained the prose of the Second Empire was becoming. Under the imperial régime, which he admitted might be the effect rather than the cause of the enervation of France that he deemed universal, but which in any case typified it, he maintained that "prose which is an art, prose which has literary pretensions, is being supplanted by prose absolutely naked which is mere writing." This state of things he would not have been surprised to learn that our own democracy, which he was pessimistically inclined to misconceive, was later—itself now more or less "imperialized"—to illustrate and even to idealize. The French however have a reliable passion for prose, as indirectly M. France attests in declaring that they do not object to poetry unless it be poetic. As to prose we are less fortunate, especially at the present day, when prose, plus the feeling that should give it style and make it art, is often popularly, though I believe less now than recently, diverted into what is called free verse; and when, following the example of a race in its childhood and civilization in its dawn, our multitude of writers so frequently begin, even in college, with poetry, and if, like Wordsworth, deserted later by the Muse, unlike him, fail to cultivate in their subsequent writing any æsthetic spirit whatever. In fine, we are to ask ourselves if prose is an art or not. If it is and is composed only of clarity and simplicity, however difficult of attainment these qualities may be, it is reasonably clear that it is a reasonably simple one. We may be sure the masters of prose found the matter more complicated, more ambitious as well as more rewarding, imposing, in fact, success in the capture of Beauty, and her imprisonment in an appropriately golden cage.

In the plastic arts there is plenty of appropriate prose which is nevertheless in its degree beautiful. Henry James happily speaks of Magdalen Tower as "that pearl of prose Gothic"; a great deal of beautiful sculpture is prose though not prosaic; similarly with painting. Indeed in painting there is only one of its various departments where poetry is obligatory, though in this one I think it should be so deemed under some effective penalty: the landscape-painter should certainly never forget that "the poetry of earth is never dead." The wisdom of protecting both poetry and prose from "prose poetry" is justified in the manifest interest of each; as a hybrid it is inevitably caricature. But poetic prose on the other hand, or for that matter poetic anything, is no more poetry than, say, a sunset is a poet. Sentiment in itself is poetic and carries its perfume with it everywhere, into prose as well as into verse. And any plea for a richer prose than that which now, as it were, scudding along under bare poles, scurries to the haven of its conclusions, one may legitimately base on the universality of sentiment—on the unity of the æsthetic element and its claims to a more extended penetration of the domain of literature.

Of recent years the striking phenomenon of the expansion of journalism has tended to obstruct this penetration, journalism not only having little weakness for the æsthetic but acting more or less on the principle expressed by French irony in the saying, *Ote-toi de là que je m'y mette.* In fact its own invasion of the domain of literature has been in such force and at so many points that one is rather driven to hope it may, like other invaders, content itself with material conquest and ultimately be assimilated by the higher civilization of the conquered. In political writing the standard of effectiveness perhaps automatically excludes the graces of expression; so far as these are in any degree excursions they must properly be suspect. So far as they may be classified under the head of fitness, however, they have obvious point, and style, being at least not an external embellishment but an inner order, appears with relevance—in, for instance, the successful simplification and calculated precision of the late Frank Cobb's daily application to current events of a pondered political philosophy. But such instances are none too frequent in the political or other fields, and as a rule the invading hosts of journalism, establishing themselves in all the border provinces of literature—notably in the much harried march of criticism—not unnaturally treat with contempt such laws and traditions of the country as hamper their rather exclusively temperamental equipment and expression. In daily journalism, the time factor is remorseless and itself trims a writer's style of superfluities, and the inescapable "Go to it" of necessity is a command carrying with it so radical an inhibition, and so strict a construction, of irrelevance as to produce in the newspaper world, in spite of salient exceptions, a general stylistic result of conspicuous bleakness. In truth, what areas of excellent writing of all kinds, since the days illumined by the sun of eloquence, have stretched their "nude and sere" expanse beneath a leaden sky and shivered in the pale diffused twilight of a wan explicitness, exhibiting with chill detachment a prospect devoid of charm! There have been, as I say, notable exceptions even in the newspaper world, but it has undeniably felt the general frost.

This widespread refrigeration set in long ago more or less coincidently, perhaps, with the rise of the Manchester school, and was very likely in some degree responsible for the dejected view Carlyle took of what he called the Dismal Science. The plantigrade tread of its resolutely inductive process might quite conceivably "get on" nerves as exposed as his. When his Reminiscences appeared—*consule Planco!*—I remember calling the acid but graphic characterization of his friend Mill's talk as "rather wintry" to the attention of the late E. L. Godkin—a Benthamite indeed in whom there was no other guile—and enjoying the latter's amused and unusual accord with the Sage of Chelsea, who (he did not believe much in sages) mostly provoked his impatience. There was nothing "wintry" about Mr. Godkin's writing any more than about his talk or himself. Arthur Sedgwick, his own style distinguished in much the same way, wrote of him: "Mr. Godkin's is what the best English has always been, pointed, strong, and simple. For lucidity and directness it is unequalled among contemporary writers in this country or in England." And he continues, as we should expect him to: "The Essays are contributions to political and economic literature of the most solid sort." However, solid political and economic literature is rarely literature so far as literature is an art, save—may one say?—in inadvertence; usually, at least, it lacks æsthetic claims and to imply that the best English has always been merely pointed, strong, simple, lucid, and direct is to imply that the English of the masters of English prose is not the best. To assert this is not to assert that their English is pointless, weak, complicated, obscure, and circuitous; only that it does something more than avoid these vices and illustrate their antithetical virtues.

This something is to illustrate the æsthetic element of style—style itself as distinct from statement, even from that rare and exemplary order of statement characterized by all the aforesaid virtues. Indeed this element also might have been pointed out in Mr. Godkin's writing. It followed rather rigidly the counsel of concealment of art by art; and its felicities are of course all the greater for being so distinctly not frippery but integral; though he certainly eschewed eloquence and his sustained pressure of order and movement followed closely the contour of the subject. His distinction lay in conceiving his subject in relation to its governing principle and threading the detail which his erudition and experience amply provided in close company with this guide. This unified his essay, or article, and made the net impression it left as definite as its title. But if as a writer he divided with Curtis the primacy among our journalists, instead of holding it unchallenged, it was, I think, because he embodied so exclusively the Emersonian ideal, "See that you hold yourself fast by the intellect." His writing avoided emotional content or color, the writer evidently considering that "all that sort of thing" so far as it could be deemed pertinent at all should go without saying, not to say be reserved for private usage—a preserve of whose inviolability to poaching he was perhaps exorbitantly jealous; which is a little curious considering his fellowship with Burke. Undoubtedly he admired Burke less for his style than for his having, as Arnold says, "saturated politics with thought." Had Godkin not in general so pointedly ignored the æsthetic element, his prose must have been more persuasive, whereas, which was surely regrettable, it was pointedly not persuasive at all. His attitude was a little that of President Seelye on beginning psychology with a new class: "I shall not ask you to believe, but defy you to deny." With maturer readers this was less effective than with undergraduates, and though Godkin's belief was undoubtedly that American newspaper readers, as well as writers, particularly lacked maturity, he hardly allowed for the fact that as to this they distinctly disagreed with him.

Since his day the press has seen great changes. Mr. Talcott Williams in his jewel of a book, "The Newspaper Man," records them impressively as well as vividly. Perhaps in segregating its juvenilia in its other columns it has given its maturity the opportunity to expand editorially as, in many admirable instances, has markedly occurred, though there were certainly giants in those days; any old newspaper man would be recreant to forget it. And development in style has scarcely kept pace with this evolution. The familiar phenomenon in old days of a beautiful piece of writing has grown notably rare, and such a figure as Mr. Kingsbury wears in consequence an air of comparative isolation and survival. With more reason than elsewhere no doubt, but still even here not a justifying amount, in journalism as well as in literature of more permanent purpose, not merely the poetic but the æsthetic element entire has often been excluded from our prose in frigid disregard of its own æsthetic tradition.

Moments when the "craze" of "æstheticism" flourished naturally did this tradition no good, and perhaps it was because, like Pre-Raphaelitism earlier, it became spent with its own extravagances, that the movement subsided, languidly resigning its torch to reactionary hands. In the sense that a man may be said to personify a movement, it may be said that Oscar Wilde extinguished the flame that Pater had lighted. Mr. Yeats says that Wilde "believed himself to value nothing but words in their emotional associations and he had turned his style to a parade as though it were his show and he Lord Mayor." As in the Restoration reaction which succeeded the Puritan orgy of asceticism, according to Arnold, people said: "This type at any rate is amiss; we are not going to be all like *that*," sunflowers or not, and followed after the prophets of a new dispensation, the prophets of the present day, Samuel Butler and Shaw. I must quote what Mr. Yeats says of them, too: "He [Shaw] was right to claim Samuel Butler for his master, for Butler was the first Englishman to make the discovery that it is possible to write with great effect without music, without style either good or bad, to eliminate from the mind all emotional implication and to prefer plain water to every vintage. . . . Presently [after attending a series of Shaw representations] I had a nightmare that I was haunted by a sewing-machine that clicked and shone, but the incredible thing was that the machine smiled, smiled perpetually." One understands Wilde's remark about Shaw, also reported by Mr. Yeats, to the effect that "he had no enemies but was much disliked by his many friends."

Clicking and glitter do vary the current clarity and simplicity on occasion but do not modify them emotionally. For such modification, once admitting the element of feeling to the realm of prose, once agreeing that prose need not always be prosaic, the most fruitful source both of inspiration and of guidance—aside from special study and attentive reading—I think myself would be fellowship with the other arts, the arts concerned with beauty as poetry is and as in the same degree and for the most part no doubt prose is not. Our ideas are perhaps not very clear on this point. Very likely it is more or less vaguely held that beauty is an abstraction which, like style, no one can adequately define; that in the prose explicitly devoted to it—as in much of the poetry and in fact a good deal of the plastic arts, up to their latest phase, at any rate—it oftenest appears as inanity; that, the masters apart, as heretofore understood and incarnated it is apt to be allied with conventionality;

and that clarity and simplicity inherently possess a superior order of it after all. On the other hand our prose, at all events, sometimes possesses more than is recognized. "Main Street," for example, so far as quality is concerned, seems to me hardly less remarkable—more so, alas, than its successor—for traces of beauty in landscape and atmosphere and other pictoriality, intimately observed and vividly recorded, than for being Main Street. Yet I do not remember hearing or seeing any notice of its containing any beauty whatever. One could hardly have a better example, if I am right about the fact, of the general insensitiveness to the æsthetic element as shown by a general failure to recognize it unprepared.

The truth is that familiarity with the æsthetic field is not as yet a part of our general culture, and until it is, prose will be the last phase of our cultivated expression to realize its potentialities of beauty and therefore of style. Phases of painting at present equally laggard are likely to be less lasting, being not so much dull to beauty as radically divorced from it and therefore promising a readier reaction. I do not mean that the fine arts have not received conspicuous attention from English and American writers of distinction in this especial field. Quite the contrary is the fact. Our museums too are multiplying, as is well known, and there are striking instances by the score of the progressive dissemination among us of the plastic arts (including, of course, architecture in the term as susceptible of "modelling" in a high degree) and eminently of music. There is, however, a tremendous numerical disproportion between our writers and, I will not say our fine-art practitioners, alone, but even our connoisseurs and professionals put together. Everyone who knows how to read and write is a partially—even though sometimes quite partially—equipped writer, whereas a difficult technic must at the outset be met and mastered in any other art. But the matter is essentially not one of numbers. Essentially it resides in the fact that the cultivated writer, as such, does not in the least feel a knowledge of æsthetic principles, data, and phenomena to be incumbent on him. With this exception *nihil humani*, so far as it comes in his way, escapes his interest or at least pointedly disengages his responsibility. But the exception has only to be pondered to appear extravagant.

Naturally, there are reasons for it. Prominent among them no doubt is the belief that the fine arts constitute an esoteric field from which the profane are warned off by the professional. This belief has been decidedly, and I should say disastrously, fostered by such artists as take their cue from Whistler's dictum that their work should be received by the public in silence—like mathematics, as Whistler said, or perhaps like medicine, a view unfavorable to its widespread absorption and rather more in accord with the initial reception of Whistler's own work by the expert "remnant" composed of his fellow-artists. His work owed the beginnings of its subsequent vogue mainly, perhaps, to the critics and connoisseurs, unless we except Whistler's own talk about it—for which everyone now can see that we ought all to be grateful. However, the professional view also seems supported by the *a priori* consideration that those who handle the tools should be the best judges of the result. The retort that to judge of an egg it is not necessary to be a hen is hardly convincing refutation, though perhaps on a level with some of the discussion. If this had not been proved interminable, the *amour propre* of each side being enlisted, one might still further suggest the well-known difficulty of judging the forest when among its trees, and the likelihood of an equally serious, not to say far more extended, lay study of results matching a superior professional concentration on process. The result of the Squeers system of learning its spelling by washing the window was the misspelling of "window," and half the expert world in the sphere of fine art can at almost any time be set against the other half on any burning question of *expertise*, the question itself only to be decided later by a general consensus including judges of greater detachment. Even if ever decided, one may add, since the courts of last resort will always be temperamentally divided.

The point mainly pertinent here is that this close corporation view operates infallibly, if insensibly, to accentuate the apathy of the generally cultivated regarding a field which the workers in it guard so jealously from trespass. The public, debarred from entering, remains cold to invitations to look over the fence—even at last, it may be, for the mere "once over" glance. The sincere belief of executants, in a necessarily narrow and "intensive" practice, that nobody else does or can know anything about it seems, moreover, as I say, logically plausible enough to persuade the public that it is sound. The public forgets that it is open to the critic to know at least all that the artist—many artists—can tell him, besides having resources of his own, and that unless silence is to be rigidly prescribed all around he is as a commentator something of an executant himself. At any rate the result of provincially forcing the esoteric note is not to quiet the critics but to estrange the public. It may be quite negligible as it affects the executant hierarchy, though one might have at least the same doubt about that as the innovating executant in his turn has about the academic. But its obvious effect on the general cultivated public is far-reaching.

And the prose writer as such, belonging essentially quite as much to the general cultivated public as to the profession of letters, so far as any technical classification distinguishes them and, as regards the fine arts, being altogether to be classed with this public, remains—in very much the proportion in which æsthetics is a sealed book to him—uninspired by the element of beauty, or, say, by a third of the ideal universe. Here and there a poet may arise destitute of acquaintance with the monumental and grandiose *corpus* of æsthetic expression that mankind began in the dawn of time and has been adding to ever since, and with its philosophy; nature may inspire as well as produce him. But the prose writer is likely to have to forego the element of beauty in some definite proportion to his ignorance of art. As regards the element of style in general (the æsthetic element in his own style so far as his workmanship is conscious art), he must be at a palpable disadvantage if his equipment is defective and his inspiration limited by the absence of that intimacy with ordered and rhythmic beauty in which all art must live in order to be living art —major or minor, great or small, poetry or prose. In any case, minus art, prose will cease to have the style which is its æsthetic element. So far as prose is concerned Mr. Middleton Murry will be quite right in saying "there are styles but no style"—a logical result of his (not very consistent) exclamation elsewhere: "As if the effort to be unmistakable were not the very secret of style!" A secret, then, one may remark, possibly possessed but certainly not disclosed by linguistic pedants—such as, for a shining example, Fitzedward Hall—in whom this effort is most unmistakable. "The true writer," Mr. Murry proceeds, "insists that the reader shall feel exactly what he intends him to feel." If the writer's effort to be unmistakable is successful the reader may have a perception the more, but how is this perception to be converted into feeling? To feel exactly what the writer intends him to feel merely because the writer makes his meaning clear would often, even if possible, be decidedly risky. He might not like the feeling. The notion is exorbitant. As a mere means of securing cogency, sufficient style to engage the emotions has its value. The most elementary rhetoric prescribes the principles of persuasion as well as those of exposition.

However, the current theory of prose style as consisting of clarity and simplicity is more modest and does not involve illusions about persuasion through anything but substance. What it does involve is, as I began by saying, a confusion of what conditions style with what constitutes it. No one would deny the claims of clarity and simplicity as conditioning elements of style. Even if its burden is rococo its own structure should be simple enough to make definite and coherent the extravagance it is designed to exhibit. But neither clarity nor simplicity is properly to be called an æsthetic element unless it be made to count as one. Neither has anything intrinsically in common with order and movement, harmony and rhythm. In literary composition, in fact, they are not so much qualities of style as of diction and phraseology. Substance once simplified, diction that is not simple lacks taste. There is no excuse for elaborating mere communication; modern euphuism anywhere is absurd. And phraseology that is not clear merely calls for clarification. But it is misleading to regard either clarity or simplicity as an æsthetic factor unless it be vivified into activity and become itself a sensuous element instead of a mere conductor, unless clarity be felt as clearness sensible, and simplicity be accented as such. To reduce style to clarity and simplicity and then reduce clarity and simplicity to imperceptibility in the interest of removing all "barriers" between writer and reader as sometimes advocated (and recently rather naïvely praised in Hudson, for instance) is, as regards style, to effect a reduction to absurdity. Style is interpretative not obstructive, but it is no more a mere vehicle than it is a barrier, and if qualities like clearness and simplicity are to replace or even to color it, they must acquire its character—its character as an element, and an æsthetic element, of expression instead of as altogether a conduit of thought. Lucidity will elucidate not less nor more but better if it is made to count as envelope and atmosphere, thus increasing the sense of the whole in the substance to be communicated—made stylistic, in a word. Clarity in a landscape-painter's technic, for example, is a lens rather than a vacuum. Its aim is not to aid the observer to scrutinize nature, but to enhance her—not being a scientific instrument but an æsthetic value; and in the same sense as that in which Arnold declares: "Truth of science does not become truth of religion till it is made religious," we may say that clarity does not become an æsthetic element until it is made æsthetic.

As to simplicity, it may very well illustrate taste without achieving style. There is more style as style, though style misplaced, in affectation than in artlessness, more—to make the French distinction that Arnold domesticated—in *simplesse* than in *simplicité*. The simplicity of Quaker costume has the effect of style only by contrasting in its rarity with the general apparel. A whole community in this tasteful garb might have order in the sense of orderliness, but its order would be inorganic and would lack movement—contrasting but tamely with, for example, the Spanish black that, even when excessive, unifies the rainbow of brilliant accentuation with which it is besprinkled, everywhere intimating the sense for style existent in Spanish carriage and character, and emergent, condensed and vivid, in Calderon and Velasquez. The Japanese practice of confining domestic decoration to one kakemono at a time in a room, though by giving relief to the picture it achieves a certain play of emphasis, should in the long run be felt as rather meagre in style. When an admirer of the Washington Monument alleged its simplicity in justification of his admiration, he evoked the suggestion that no monument would be still simpler. The Greek "nothing too much" is a counsel of taste, and as applied to style should be supplemented by a caution against nothing at all. Leopold Eidlitz, to whom the Victorian architecture of New York owed so much, offered, when the Brooklyn Bridge was building, to make the towers architectural. At the time, public opinion would have sustained the official declination he met with, and the bridge remains the strictly engineering monument it was then considered and considered preferable to have it. Eidlitz was a native of Prague and would perhaps have given New York something comparable to the Karlsbrücke towers, not as appropriate as the Pont Alexandre III is to Paris, nor as splendid, but in any case a monument of style which it is still exasperating to remember we have lost. As it is, we have the simplicity of masonry as masonry to console us. Subversive as the fact may be of Ruskin's theory of art, the cave as a place of worship, even if in given instances it have more beauty, has undoubtedly less style though more simplicity than the cathedral. The simplicity of the nude in art should surely have style, but I imagine that the nude in life is apt to lack it. Perhaps devotees of simplicity at all hazards are so sweeping because in all deliberate art they scent affectation. But such timidity is in this category of circumstances too preponderantly moral. There is, plainly, simplicity and simplicity. That which is the result of simplification is quite different from either monotony or the miscellaneity that is practically undifferentiated—a principle scrupulously observed by the modern "window-dresser" in whose art style, too often rejected of other builders, finds a welcome refuge. The academic haberdasher whose "correct apparel" is instinct with style that is standard, is his congenial ally. New York, accordingly, particularly Fifth Avenue, owes to both a debt larger than is generally recognized.

As an achievement—during which it acquires its style—simplicity has quite other sanctions than the originally meagre. Exiguity of expression may give substance a salience of contrast equivalent to that of the emphasis of energy, but no more than this converse excess is blankness properly to be called style. Saint-Gaudens's statue in the Washington cemetery which has fully as much style as the more complicated work more instinctive with him when he was not, as it were, working in unison with artists of the strain of LaFarge and Henry Adams—and they newly returned from the Land of Nirvana—gets its style from its simplification. There is nothing simple in its conception any more than artless in its inspiration. Simplicity and the mystic or even the mysterious are mutually antithetical. The celebrated pentameter,

"A Mr. Wilkinson, a clergyman,"

in parody of Wordsworth's simplicity, attributed to Fitzgerald, has a certain effect of style because it is, contrariwise, *simplesse*—Tennysonian simplicity, one may say, remembering Arnold's citation of "Dora" as an example of the quality. What it parodies, indeed, is less the poet's poetry than his simplicity in deeming poetry that which but for his theory he would have seen as prose. Thus even subtleties as well as broader relevancies substantiate the quite radical distinction between simple simplicity and style. And just as clarity is only to be made æsthetic by density sufficient to render it perceptible, æsthetic simplicity must be the result of simplification in the treatment, given complexity in the theme.

One can, in fancy, see miscellaneity acquire style in the actual process of being simplified. One can, in fact, see in "modern art" the process itself apparently arrested for inspection often on the hither side of any result—other than the half-way effect of simplification proceeding, instead of either style achieved or simplicity attained. The notablest effects of the kind are reached in sculpture, perhaps, and by a reversal of the Beaux-Arts technic of proceeding from the general to the particular. That of Elie Nadelmann has sometimes more than a theoretic interest—though plainly less for others than for the enthusiastic artist himself. Of course simplification may be carried so far as out of mere momentum to o'erleap style, as it were, and alight, a little dazed, in featureless simplicity. On the other hand a theme may be too simple to simplify. People speak of simplicity as if in itself it were an æsthetic value, like size. Size includes its corollary, scale, and though even without scale it is often extremely impressive—its impressiveness as a compositional effect is due less to the artist than to our creating a relation by unconsciously assuming our own scale as an element of contrast, and any relation is a rudiment of style. I remember someone speaking of the impressiveness of the old Mullet post-office at Broadway and Park Row to Eidlitz, who replied that a pile of barrels of the same dimensions would have more—conveying, as unminimized by senseless modelling, a more unmixed sense of the superiority of size. Thus, possibly, the Pyramids—mountains, certainly—"lord it o'er us," as Sterling says is the Dædalian way.

However, featureless simplicity—either implicit in the theme or the result of exaggerated simplification—clearly can't be helped out in this way. Like clarity, simplicity must itself actively contribute to that sense of the whole which it is also the function of style to accentuate in the parts. Converted into active values, both perform a stylistic as well as a rhetorical service in illuminating and vivifying those intrinsic constituents of style in the abstract, order and movement, harmony and rhythm. But surely neither their utility as rhetorical fundamentals, nor their stylistic value, once transformed from conditions into constituents of style, is impeached by denying their entire and exclusive sufficiency for a prose ideal that need in nowise exclude them in including the element of beauty as well. In fine, if prose is an art and not merely a craft, one of the essentials of prose style is beauty. Conversely, certainly, any prose of which the burden is, even remotely, related to *belles-lettres* is irrefutably irrelevant in so far as it is not art, and unless it be science. But I think one may go farther and maintain that all prose in so far as it is *literature* is entitled to some measure of beauty and bound to the requirements of art—in which blend of privilege and obligation it is best sustained by the inspiration, and best forwarded by the guidance, of the genius of style.

IV

ENGLISH PROSE TRADITION

It is singular that the claims of the element of beauty to count as a force in English letters should not to-day be more widely and cordially recognized in view of the unquestioned tradition of distinctly æsthetic English prose. This tradition has been handed on from one exceptional writer to another in a line curiously paralleling that of the general evolution of our prose into its present prim and prosaic, clear and simple, medium of communication. But one must acknowledge nevertheless that aggrandizement of simplicity and clarity as qualities of ideal prose style has strong historic warrant as well as intrinsic appeal. English prose did not extricate itself from poetry without a struggle, and a struggle during which it was necessary to insist on these qualities as conditions of its individuality, of its *raison d'être* as prose, but a struggle also traces of which it still shows. It lost style as it acquired taste. At least its style, in gaining order, lost movement. Johnson's stateliness is static beside Milton's, however indubitably inorganic Milton's inexorable continuity. Moreover, as Balzac says, "where form dominates, sentiment disappears," and the Augustan age did not succeed in establishing the formal standards set by Dryden, Defoe, and Swift without sacrificing its sentiment, even in its poetry, and of course more notably still in its prose. After Donne's, Dryden's rational and regular prose, however spirited, rather lowers the curtain on the romantic. Defoe's after Sir Thomas Browne's is Amsterdam after Venice. Swift's is in somewhat different case. His irony is plainly an active æsthetic element, and, permeating the directness and precision of his style, makes it a miracle considered as a vehicle for his bitter genius, though as a medium his manner allowed it no warmth. But, a prophet in his own country, his environment was too close to him to find in it aught beyond the directness and precision it was already set to follow, and, thus, failed to note that his simplicity is more highly organized than superficially appears. Writing of Voltaire Mr. Gamaliel Bradford observes that of his style "unfailing clarity, absolute precision and exactitude are a small part," and he continues: "Beyond these there is a subtle secret of rhythm especially, such as Swift had, a power of adapting all the cunning possibilities of utterance to the thing to be uttered, of bringing out the infinite resources of words in color and accent," etc. The characterization is perhaps a shade enthusisatic for Swift, but it is altogether inapplicable to Defoe or even Addison and serves excellently to emphasize the relief of Swift's eminence in style as one facet of the figure of which Thackeray said: "The giants must live apart. The kings can have no company."

Rather than Swift's example it is perhaps more particularly the days and nights devoted to the study of Addison, following Johnson's counsel, that have resulted in ridding prose of the purple patch—admirable achievement, to be sure—but also in extracting its color. The prose of Bacon and Milton, of Donne and Browne, of Jeremy Taylor, of Clarendon—was it necessary to jettison all that nobility to get rid of grandiloquence? If prose poetry is primitive and its satisfactions are crude, which is certainly true, was the only alternative prosaic prose? There is naturally no gain without some loss, but in this case has not the loss been needlessly excessive? It is no doubt a great gain to have secured a medium in which the grammarian can converse with the grocer, and Bacon's "Essays" recast in the diction of Freeman, or even one still more strictly familiar, would advantageously popularize much wisdom. But it is surely possible to pay too high a price for such Benthamite blessings. Moreover, they are so apt to come about of themselves, utility being the main principle of natural selection, that it is superfluous to preach them and fatuous to plume ourselves on their possession, as is now so generally done, out of due proportion and in neglect of their cost. "The world has grown grey from thy breath" might have been addressed by the poet to the utilitarian spirit with far greater reason than to the source to which the elevated uses of the world owe their suffusion with the emotion that crystallized the world's spiritual elevation into conduct.

No doubt the rise, triumph, and subsequent sway of natural science, which calls chiefly for exposition—heedless of Ruskin's desire to inoculate it with reverence!—has had a powerful indirect influence in establishing our prose standard, having considerably taken over the field of history, for one example. Another instance, more pointed and also more general in scope, is the fact that, through Herbert Spencer science has itself expounded style, thus directly popularizing the precision and directness fully adequate to its own uses. But the whole trend of modern general tendency has been to exalt unemotional prose in theory, and to confine practice within its limits, illustrating, and content with illustrating, the virtues of clarity and simplicity. Taste has developed in this direction and it would very likely be temerarious to assert that it could, up to date, have functioned more wisely than by functioning in the negative way of discountenancing defects rather than in encouraging virtues. In extending its province, the spread of democracy has of itself restricted its operation, rendering this largely rudimentary. The inculcations of culture must wait till its inhibitions are assimilated. Before the potentialities of prose are realized its limitations are to be learned, and appreciation of its character must precede the exploitation of its capacities.

Any illustrative reference to the evolution of our English prose tradition as bearing on prose theory would naturally therefore begin in this way, by noting preliminarily the elimination in prose of its surviving surplusage of unassimilated poetic amalgam obstructing its own flow and confusing its own order. It would thereupon naturally proceed to magnify the prose resulting from this purification as first exhibited on a general scale in the Augustan age. And its own logic would tempt it to ascribe the faults of Augustan literature, finding none in its style, to its substance. This is the line that, in fact, Arnold followed and the conclusion he reached. And, as his exposition of prose theory, which I have already described as having done more than any other to define the limitations and indicate the character of prose, is nevertheless marked by a tendency to establish its non-poetic character a little too rigidly and thereby render it prosaic, so his practical conclusion, in the matter of the tradition, that the literature of our great prose age was "second-rate and provincial" in spite of an unimpeachable style, seems to me rather literal logic. The author of "The English Humourists of the Eighteenth Century" would perhaps have raised his eyebrows at the conclusion, and I think it would be easy to contest the premises by maintaining that Augustan style had a good deal to do with such inferiority as Arnold felt in the literature. Was there in fact anywhere any great preoccupation with prose style itself—beyond the systematizing of syntax and the rudiments of rhetoric? Certainly nothing on the plane of elevated consideration shown by Donne in his remarkable sermon on the style of the Scriptures, ascribing it as well as their substance to the inspiration of the Holy Ghost. "If we would take," says Donne, "all those Figures and Tropes which are collected out of secular Poets and Orators we may give higher and livelier examples of every one of those Figures out of the Scriptures than out of all the Greek and Latin Poets and Orators; and they mistake it much that thinke that the Holy Ghost hath rather chosen a low and barbarous and homely style than an eloquent and powerful manner of expressing himself." And, more analytically, in another discourse: "The Holy Ghost is an eloquent Author, a vehement and an abundant Author but yet not luxuriant; he is far from a penurious, but as far from a superfluous style, too." Addison, indeed!

The law of reaction operates as regularly in literature as in the life of which literature, as the expression, follows the impulse, and the age of prose quite inescapably turned prosaic when its turn came. Beauty's lines settled into primness; brilliance, become general, made paste popular; art lost its independent inspiration in adaptation to the mode. Congreve succeeded to Herrick, Pope replaced Donne. When the Town developed its tyranny, style in prose sacrificed its own state to society. Order was pattern and movement a minuet. Intelligence gave no quarter to the affections; Steele is the only writer of the age who eminently had heart. Everybody wrote well—as today; but—also as today—without that tincture of emotion that warms and lifts adequate utterance into æsthetic correspondence with the substance uttered. In fine, the age itself, surcharged with manner, formal or familiar, formalized style. Its taste stanched its sentiment, and style without sentiment is music for the deaf. On the other hand, from the point of view of substance it seems to me much more can be said for it. Certainly we may say that its style, which made its prose easy reading, is not what makes it always read and read again. In the next age, at all events, prose regained, also in reaction, its ceremony with Johnson and its pageantry with Burke.

I have said that the inhibitions of Arnold's doctrine were particularly fruitful, but it is also true that his intimations were not universally approved in all their strictness, and that his readers differed a good deal in their ability to follow his applications in their full explicitness. They are to be taken no doubt as literature, not dogma. They were in nowise dogmatically proclaimed. But even his followers felt less interest in the didactic than in the purely critical implications of his views, and were more concerned with their suggestiveness and soundness than with their universal imperative; and with their contemporary pertinence rather than with their prophetic importance for the guidance of posterity. If he was too anxious to rescue for poetry some of Ruskin's prose, his suggestion nevertheless disclosed the weakness of Ruskin's emotional effusion. Prose of the centre rather than of the circumference was no doubt the aim, and Bossuet's stylistic rhetoric fitting garb for significant and striking intellectual perceptions and conclusions—and even Thiers, who nevertheless had his own kind of fatuity, furnished a commendable contrast to the personal caprice of Kinglake or the mannered brilliance of Macaulay. But while it was true that no one had treated the general subject critically with such stimulating success, it was perfectly plain that the "Essays in Criticism," the "Lectures on Translating Homer," "The Study of Celtic Literature" were not merely in this respect so many post-graduate text-books but the ranking literary literature of their period as well, and that the prose they practised excelled the precision they preached.

Arnold himself had not always written verse when lyrically inspired—he who so eminently could when so minded! Witness, for a single instance, the apostrophe to Oxford—illuminating example of eloquent and elevated fervor, style vibrant with personal feeling, yet perfectly subdued to that conjoined restraint of feeling and freedom of gesture, that fusion of meaning addressed to the reason with the emotion awakened by the beauty and truth thus specifically declared, which is, though surely not prose poetry, as surely poetic prose. And it would be easy, as at this date it should be superfluous, to cite passages in practically parallel vein throughout the works of this admirable prose artist. But what his style illustrates, in abundance and with precision, that is particularly germane to the matter of English prose tradition, is the transformation of the conditioning elements of clarity and simplicity into constituting factors by saturating clarity with color, and accentuating simplicity by making it organic instead of uniform, and giving it a physiognomy as well as a silhouette. It illustrates this so strikingly in fact as, on occasion—rare occasion—to caricature it; caricature clarity, at all events, by veritably implacable iteration. More and more the burden of his prose has come to be part of our general thinking and feeling, and people hold his views and writers parrot his phrases with so secure a sense of accord as to have an obscure sensation of ownership, not to say the illusion of origination. Such a result in itself contributes to the tradition a demonstration that prose is not merely an art, but as much an art as any other.

And the echoes of "Essays in Criticism" were

still vibrating and its counsels in everyone's mind when, a decade or so later, Pater's "Studies in the Renaissance" appeared, and without essentially or precisely modifying the "Essays," unveiled a new point of view, one less strict and more sensuous. Preaching by example, at least, the "Studies" gave renewed sanction to the element of style touched with emotion in English prose. Style touched with emotion may very well be the defining characteristic of what is to be called æsthetic as distinguished from plain prose, the words being used as strictly as those of Arnold's famous formula of religion being morality touched with emotion; that is to say, the emotion being that evoked as the style itself is forged in the writer's heat and hammered on the anvil of his concentrated thought, as well as that inspired by the substance it arms and fortifies. Thackeray must have had over his style many moments when he felt as he did over his inspiration of making Rebecca admire her husband in spite of her own difficulties, when he struck the table with his fist, exclaiming: "That was a stroke of genius." Every writer consciously a writer must, in his own degree and fatuity aiding, have had analogous experiences. Assuredly Pater did not invent æsthetic prose, but very definitely he underlined it. This he did, not only through the detachment of a higher relief and a richer color than the style of the English essay had ever known, but by a franker concentration on this abstract element, thus disengaged and rendered concrete, to an extent that brought it immensely into the foreground. The reader's attention in turn became concentrated on the author, "burning," to borrow his own figure, with his "hard gemlike flame." This did not in the "Studies" distract one from their substance—the author was too obviously as well as too subtly identified with the substance, almost as novel among us in the seventies as the style. No one who "discovered" Pater in those days will have forgotten the experience. Style introducing art, through the medium of beauty common to both, was a memorable transaction. I can still hear at will the chanting tones of Montgomery Schuyler, our bookish hierophant, reading aloud to our Saturday afternoon group in the *World* office of those days, the honey-dripping cadences, the stately strophes, celebrating the loveliness of the School of Giorgione. Later came "Marius the Epicurean" and established in many quarters the cult of Pater.

The desultory remarks that Mr. Yeats lets fall about style in his reminiscences are often, as I have already shown, so suggestive as to make one wish they were a little systematized. One of them records that a few years ago he had re-read "Marius," expecting to find that he cared for it no longer; "but," he says, "it still seemed to me, as I think it seemed to us all, the only great prose in modern English." Many readers, however, could not hold the pose and fell away. To speak a little in the vein of the period, the "cause" of English æsthetic prose suffered a reaction. One recalls the slight feeling of relief experienced when that *enfant terrible* of the expiring Victorian age, Mr. Max Beerbohm, now nearly thirty years ago, made public confession and avoidance beginning as follows: "Not that even in those more decadent days of my childhood [five years before, when he was a freshman at Oxford] did I admire the man as a stylist. Even then I was angry that he should treat English as a dead language, bored by that sedulous ritual wherewith he had laid out every sentence as in a shroud—hanging long over its marmoreal beauty or ever he could lay it at length in his book, its sepulchre." Obviously Mr. Beerbohm was still under the spell. In spite of these brave words it is evident from them that the fascination of still earlier days at school when he "had read 'Marius the Epicurean' in bed with a dark lantern" still remained. *Nemo repente est* faithless to early loves. But it may be doubted if "Marius" has not on the whole taken its permanent place in the literary pantheon in virtue of being a great book rather than great prose. Its style forced the note of style. It got between the reader and the book, displacing what it aimed to exhibit. Such divorce of substance and style is far from uncommon. Poise between them is as difficult to achieve as either style or substance by itself; especially when the artist is initiating a "movement" in favor of one of them. Moreover, if Pater's style possessed great beauty, it lacked accent. Many disciples must have found the posthumous fragment, "Gaston de Latour," unreadable. Still, if one shrinks a little from a surfeit, one feels graceless when long passages of "Marius" recur to the memory; that at the close of the book, for example, where the atmosphere, one would say, is at first everything, but where one soon perceives that the soft radiance suffusing it is in such harmony with the substance it illumines as to sublimate the union of the two into the closest unison. To exact transmutation into poetic form of such prose would be pure formalism.

An earlier example of prose style which is so clearly æsthetic prose as almost to beguile the reader's attention from the subject is Newman's. It seems to celebrate the subject rather than expound it, as a song does its words. It has exacted a nearly unanimous tribute from critics and it is perhaps the clearest instance in English of that continuity which sometimes seems so much the inner essential trait of style as to stand in full equivalence for style itself, when it undulates in pitch and period through such sustained passages as those of Newman. Employed in controversy, as in the "Apologia," its air of almost saintly detachment has, or had, so captivating an effect as, quite apart from the argument, to make the reader a willing convert. On the other hand it seemed in general so far away from the stress and variety of life and reality, the multifarious concerns of any active reader, so merely musical a murmur, so smoothly flowing a current, that what it said or sang or carried appeared to lose its character as a message and be lulled out of any very momentous meaning. The message perhaps was adapted to the style, not of necessity in being doctrinally "impossible," as Arnold called it, and therefore counting for us mainly as a medium for its own literary expression, but certainly in confining itself so largely to historic ecclesiastical and theological themes, under the ribs of which even the theory of evolutionary theology could not put a soul of widespread interest to modern men of many minds. Matter of tougher fibre would have called for a style of greater vigor than one marked by those "subtle, sweet, mournful" accents that Arnold praised, but happily for us, never emulated—even in his poetry.

These two illustrious writers aside (and perhaps one should add Landor, so monumentally "marmoreal" and De Quincey, so elaborately exalted) there are, I imagine, few moderns of unquestioned eminence in whose prose style the æsthetic element can be found too steadily salient, too persistently dominant. Here and there, it is true, this element, though decidedly present, is decidedly not always handled to the best advantage. The prose of Carlyle and Ruskin, for example, "those two grand mannerists upon whom the literature of our neighbors," says Scherer, "so mistakenly plumes itself," is largely responsible for so acid a judgment—if not indeed for their frequent association, though this was, rather vaingloriously, vaunted by Ruskin himself on other grounds. One can hardly call æsthetic in the usual sense a prose which a critic of Scherer's sobriety can call "a conscious, wilful, calculated jargon," and the author of which has the contempt that Carlyle, willing that the devil should "fly away with" them, showed for the fine arts. But Carlyle's prose is indubitably quick with the sensibility originally intended by the word æsthetic, and instinct with feeling always as genuine as its envelope is often perverse and occasionally grotesque. And for pure expression, for style impregnated with "manner and personality" truly protean, heroic, and even grandiose, as well as pathetic and even plaintive, style mirroring the mood rather more than subserving the mind, there is, one feels at times, no prose to match it. On the other hand Arnold selects as his purest and most beautiful prose the Youth's dirge over Mignon in his translation of "Wilhelm Meister," a decade before he had invented what Scherer calls his "jargon." And if later the earlier beauty and purity were thus sacrificed to the essentially, however brilliantly, artificial, it was doubtless because as he went on he fitted his form to his extravagances of feeling with less and less thought of the qualities of purity and beauty in the abstract. Ruskin's excesses are less defects of style than of personality, manner, mannerism—as Scherer says—becoming thus defects of *his* style in the gross. The formal element of *style* in his style is very generally beautifully handled, especially its movement. Intemperance is rather a moral than a technical æsthetic delinquency and though it not rarely characterizes his expression its effect chiefly is to compromise his taste, not to lessen his devotion to style. In such passages as, for instance, the rhapsody over the church and square of San Marco, certainly his style riots in exuberance, but its excess is that of feeling catching up and whirling in accelerating momentum the order and movement of his periods. Style, in a word, which is Carlyle's none too well-treated slave is his over-indulgent master. Detachment is the leaven *par excellence* that as writing his writing needs—to say nothing of the general expediency of having a little of everything in order to achieve perfect perfection! But defective æsthetic process does not discredit the values of æsthetic qualities as such, either in the abstract or, where these values are sound and keep their place, in the concrete. Certainly the ideal of æsthetic prose is not invalidated by its practice, either exaggerated as so often it appears in Ruskin or eccentric as so largely it figures in Carlyle.

In the prose of Burke and in that of Gibbon, too, the æsthetic element does keep its place. Though marked it is ancillary and the stylistic attitude of the writer is immaculate. The style is integral rather than integumental on the one hand and yet in itself objectively envisaged, with its ideal function in mind, instead of inspired by a surrender to impulse and personal expansion. At moments it may be felt to fringe the artificial, but the fact that it often has the air of being express rather than instinctive is no impeachment of its genuineness, and it is naïve to expect all traces of artifice to escape scrutiny in an art so plainly involving the taking of thought as the art of prose composition. In prose composition the only alternative to the careful is the slipshod. Even if the composer's æsthetic consecration is conspicuous rather than completely concealed, it is generally satisfactory as long as from the thought it carries it does not filch primacy for itself. Naturally in such a case one would savor a little more finesse; but this is a relative world and if in any art the essential interrelations of its elements are soundly established, hypercriticism is overweening.

Gibbon's devotion to style was conspicuous, but it was, I fancy, extremely fortunate. Professors of rhetoric will perhaps hesitate to prescribe emulation of it to any of their pupils save those who may have in view anything as important as the "Decline and Fall." Perhaps no writer could sustain so monumental a work through such a succession of grandiose phases *without* preliminary provision of a style commensurate with its proportions and significance, a style bound to seem artificial when considered in connection with common needs and uses. Even so, Gibbon himself, placid and persistent as he was, found the strain too great. Horace Walpole, as I have recalled, noted a decided falling off in subsequent volumes from the standard of the "enamelled" first. But the momentum was great enough to preserve the interest which would have disappeared without it, in spite of the material, and Carlyle's "splendid bridge from the old world to the new" reached its farther shore still retaining vastly more than the mere remains of its initial splendor.

And in the æsthetic strain I have been rather arbitrarily skeletonizing in our English prose tradition, together with Burke and Gibbon, Landor and De Quincey, Carlyle and Ruskin, Newman, Arnold, and Pater, no one would deny a place to other modern figures of undeniable eminence—*imprimis*, no doubt, Macaulay and Thackeray. Macaulay is always cited as a model of clearness, and most justly. But there are other clear writers and clearness is as elementary as, conjoined with any depth, it is difficult. Macaulay's famous style certainly had style in a marked degree, but its order and movement were so concentrated on point as quite measurably to overlook sensuousness. They appeared therefore, after all, as rhetoric, which is to style inspired by the genius of style, as skill to art. His purple patches are fully salient enough, but rather in chiaroscuro than in color. Besides, they rhapsodize the theme rather than beautify the treatment—after the manner of the canticle rather than that of the ode, one may say—and consequently as style illustrate a taste too primitive to be otherwise than primitively æsthetic. The genius of Macaulay integrates the two in such manner as to exact for his style more than a fair share of the effect of his substance, always nevertheless notably effective. His true distinction is signalized in Thackeray's tribute: "He reads twenty books to write a sentence; he travels a hundred miles to make one line of description." Such opulence was too tempting for a rhetorician to forego its exploitation. But the use he made of it to qualify as a master of style as well as of scholarship made him a glorious text-book as well as a classic. His purple patches were therefore on the one hand prodigiously, even enthusiastically "packed" and fairly vibrant with erudition made exoteric—refreshing reversal of the erudite type!—at the same time that their "tigers and camelopards bounded in the Flavian amphitheatre" to the delight more particularly of his own schoolboy; the schoolboy within us all, the schoolboy who will doubtless still exist in undiminished vigor to greet the traveller from New Zealand on his arrival to sketch from a broken arch of London Bridge the ruins of St. Paul's. But in Macaulay's own Scotch spirit we may laud the extraordinary utility if not the æsthetic fastidiousness of his style and indeed go so far as to commend it to writers of our own time who may happen equally to deserve Thackeray's eulogy.

Thackeray's own incomparable style is all the most austere pedant could ask in respect of simplicity and clarity, but it is made what it is by the infusion of these with a personal manner of such marked æsthetic quality—germs of which are manifest enough in his verses if not very salient in his drawings, but which come to full development only in his prose—as wonderfully to enrich his clarity and simplicity, and in fact to convert those qualities into something far more intricately *sui generis* than the most complicated and ornate rococo. No prose so conceals art so consummate. Its clarity involves no sacrifice of subtlety and its simplicity is the very genius of simplification. In sustained passages his prose is, in this respect, supreme; but take the first sentence that comes under one's hand—this, on Congreve: "A touch of Steele's tenderness is worth all his finery; a flash of Swift's lightning, a beam of Addison's pure sunshine, and his tawdry playhouse taper is invisible." Obviously its style makes it a language new and beautiful, as unlike everyday English as a different idiom.

Modern writers, too, less central in the stream of the tradition here, less noteworthy as being substantially of minor importance compared with the major prose succession, have nevertheless even more pointedly served the ideal of æsthetic rather than that of prosaic prose. Passages taken almost at random from Mrs. Browning's essay on the Greek Christian poets, recall the days of prose eloquence as vividly as Macaulay. This, for example, on the language which has with us so largely ceased to be even "a college fetich":

"No other language has lived so long and died so hard —pang by pang, each with a dolphin color—yielding reluctantly to that doom of death and silence which must come at last to the speaker and the speech. It is wonderful to look back and listen. Blind Homer spoke this Greek after blind Demodocus, with a quenchless light about his brows, which he felt through his blindness. Pindar rolled his chariots in it, prolonging the clamor of the games. Sappho's heart beat through it and heaved up the world's. Æschylus strained it to the stature of his high thoughts. Plato crowned it with his divine peradventures. Aristophanes made it drunk with the wine of his fantastic merriment. The later Platonists wove their souls away in it, out of sight of other souls. The first Christians heard in it God's new revelation, and confessed their Christ in it from the suppliant's knee, and presently from the bishop's throne. To all times, and their transitions, the language lent itself."

The same strain sounding in this rhapsody of the "fair-coined soul that lay rusting in a pool of tears" and that "Browning stooped and picked up," as Francis Thompson said, is to be heard in Thompson's own impassioned eulogy of Shelley, of which the following outburst must have established the new record in prose outbursts that it probably continues to hold:

"He is still at play, save only that his play is such as manhood stops to watch, and his playthings are those which the gods give their children. The universe is his box of toys. He dabbles his fingers in the day-fall. He is gold-dusty with tumbling amidst the stars. He makes bright mischief with the moon. The meteors nuzzle their noses in his hand. He teases into growling the kenneled thunder, and laughs at the shaking of its fiery chain. He dances in and out of the gates of heaven; its floor is littered with his broken fancies. He runs wild over the fields of ether. He chases the rolling world. He gets between the feet of the horses of the sun. He stands in the lap of patient Nature and twines her loosened tresses after a hundred wilful fashions, to see how she will look nicest in his song."

Undeniably such fervor "dates." And I am far from wishing that the whirligig of time might bring it about again even if it brought also writers able, as it were, to bend the same bow. Like Macaulay's it celebrates—incenses, in fact—its subject, instead of developing it. The censer however is swung by poetic, rather than purely rhetorical, sentiment, and the acolytes being poets, as Macaulay was so far from being—especially when in metre he especially tried to be—are perhaps to that extent culpable for blending *genera*. Nevertheless the result outranks rules, and feeling thus expressed is conveyed in too full measure to cause us to desire its suppression. It is feeling flowering in disciplined decorum and moving us through its consonant style as well as through its fervor. If it is tagged with a different taste from ours of today, it has all the same its lesson for our own prose in just this regard. The liberal dietitian authorizes an occasional debauch—now and then a lump of sugar, once in a while a pinch of salt. The weakness of this strain in prose, whether rhetorical or poetic or both, is a certain quality of externality inseparable from the attitude of the writer. This is, artistically considered, a manifest attitude of detachment almost in proportion as, otherwise than artistically, it is partisan, producing, also, the impression that what is being communicated has already been, rather than is being, created—a kind of chewing of the cud of classic taste instead of origination. It is exclamatory rather than expressive, with the effect of heat not light. Its style accordingly is applied rather than formative, frankly constructed decoration not decoratively constructive.

But that this attitude and character are not of necessity involved in the expression of feeling in prose, and of feeling as regards treatment not less than theme, not only appears in the style of the major masters, but far from occasionally in that of figures less commanding but of the truest distinction in the world of letters. An exceptional example is that of the late F. W. H. Myers, whose "Essays Classical" and "Essays Modern," published in the eighties of the last century, undoubtedly still keep in the esteem of all who then or thereafter made their acquaintance an altogether special place. Observe how different from Mrs. Browning's rhapsody—different with a family difference but still a palpable one—is this passage from the essay on Virgil, dealing with the same theme: the Greek language. Note its intellectual factor as the structure and its fervor as the decorative element of the passage, and mark how its eloquence permeates critical penetration instead of gilding the refined gold resplendent on the shining surface of the subject:

"There never has been, there never will be, a language like the dead Greek. For Greek had all the merits of other tongues without their accompanying defects. . . . But it was an instrument beyond the control of any but its creators. When the great days of Greece were past it was the language which made speeches and wrote books and not the men. Its French brilliancy taught Isocrates to polish platitude into epigram; its German profundity enabled Lycophron to pass off nonsense as oracles; its Italian flow encouraged Apollonius Rodius to shroud in long-drawn sweetness the languor of his inventive soul. There was nothing except the language left. Like the golden brocade in a queen's sepulchre, its imperishable splendor was stretched stiffly across the skeleton of a life and thought which inhabited there no more."

And as perfect illustrations of prose style, not suggestive of prose poetry, but, on the one hand, of prose suffused with feeling subdued to the service of style, and, on the other, of the genius of style so informing a sustained sequence of noble thought and refined emotion as to endue it throughout with a definite æsthetic element, consider the following sentences from the same essay:

"In literature as in life affection and reverence may reach a point which disposes to silence rather than to praise. . . . Yet possibly if his [the admirer's] admiration has notoriously been shared for nineteen centuries by all whose admiration was best worth having, he may venture to attempt to prove the world right where others have attempted the bolder task of proving it mistaken; or rather, if the matter in question be one by its very nature incapable of proof, he may without presumption restate in terms adapted to modern readers the traditional judgments of sixty generations of men."

And this *obiter dictum* later in the essay, briefer, but equally marked by perfection:

"It is not always at a man's crowning moment that his destiny and his duty close; and for those who fain had perished with what they held most dear, fate may reserve a more tedious trial and the sad triumphs of a life whose sun has set."

Nor is it necessary either to confine illustration of æsthetic English prose tradition to heightened expression of an elevated imaginative mood, or to seek it so far back as even the last century. The current product might be winnowed for it with the result of a reasonably rich residue. My only contention is that this residue might be richer still—far richer—and would be if the ideal of it, instead of a rigidly and pedantically prosaic ideal, were more general. Only the other day, it seems, contemporary English letters suffered the irreparable loss of a brilliant exponent of æsthetic prose theory and practice in the death of Maurice Hewlett. His distinguished series of romances needed no addition for a complete critical induction as to his contribution to the art of fiction, but the last volume he published, "Extemporary Essays," the

preface of which is dated September, 1922, is eloquent in suggestion of his having reached a period of ripeness, of reflection, of knowledge irradiating wisdom, charmingly fitted for a crepuscular career of commentary on the art of literature, with the documents of which he was saturated, and with the principles as well as the practice of which he had obviously long been preoccupied. From this volume I can cite precisely the passage I need to exemplify incontestably pure prose—prose ostensibly indeed almost as casual as that of a typical book notice—nevertheless prose so impregnated with the spirit of style expressed in the language of literature as immensely to reinforce the plain facts, simply stated, not only with a romantic atmosphere revealing the intrinsic interest of these but with a classic accompaniment of indirect allusion relating them to the stored treasures of culture. Naturally, for the full appreciation of such a passage *some* acquaintance with these treasures is necessary. But where is the logic of writing for those who, never reading, can hardly be expected to read what one writes even if, writing exclusively for their benefit he sacrifices the interest of those preferring an educated idiom? Hewlett is perhaps a shade bookish, but the trait has become so rare as to be welcome in greater excess than his. Besides, he is so clever

about it that those who would resent, will hardly discover, the tendency. Here he is writing a half dozen pages of book review and begins with this paragraph:

"Serious intention has combined with happy memories to make Mrs. Stirling's "Memoir of William and Evelyn De Morgan" a beautiful book. For the De Morgans were lovely in their lives and in death not long divided. Few such wedded pairs have shone, like a constellation, upon a naughty world. No doubt but there are plenty of them with a more local beam. But such households are hidden from the main of us. We may come upon them—to pursue the figure—unawares when we are groping in the dark, a mild and steady radiance illuminating some inches of a mossy bank. But the De Morgans shone above the hiving streets. One could steer by them, if need were. And one did. There, beyond these voices, there was peace. The book therefore preserves a valuable thing. It might easily have been spoiled in the doing; yet because it has been done with great simplicity, it could hardly have been better done."

"Extemporary Essays" is also a beautiful book and all the essays "were written for and published in daily newspaper or weekly or monthly review." They were accordingly journalism, but, continues the preface: "Rightly or wrongly they were to be literature as well as journalism" and "No man needs be the worse journalist for taking immense pains to be something beside." This it is to

have an education—a real one—to have the heart of a poet, to have the love of beauty and the sense of style, and consciously to take "immense pains" in the specific business of weaving them all into a prose that is at once exquisite and exquisitely in character, as far removed from the prosaic and pedestrian as it is abounding in the admirable relevancies of its own art. Do they order this business better in England also as well as in France? No doubt Hewlett was an exceptional journalist!—was in fact an exceptional writer in any kind—in his own country. We have ourselves exceptional writers. We have exceptional journalists too. But have we our proportional quota of exceptions? And if so, do they, if journalists, take "immense pains to be something beside"; and do they, though not journalists, betray in general a conviction that taking "immense pains" is equally essential to the writing of any prose that, possessing requisite qualities of substance, is properly to be called literature precisely because it is not properly to be called prosaic. In any case any prose writer among us plainly has the torch of a long and continuing tradition to light his footsteps if, conceiving prose as an art rather than merely as a medium, he desires to follow in the path that it illumines—and transfigures.

V

PRESENT-DAY USES—SOCIAL AND PERSONAL

In contrast to the romantic element in our prose tradition and in spite of a considerable element of the rococo recently acquired by the general taste as well as exhibited in the realm of art, our present-day æsthetic inertia, which, inculcating the virtues of simplicity without accent and clarity without color, has tended to denude our prose of æsthetic quality, operates in the same way in other fields of expressional activity. Elsewhere and much more seriously than in our prose does the moral as well as the æsthetic sense miss the influence, at once bracing and seductive, of the element of style. Distinctly through its appeal to the disposition to relax rather than to stiffen, into which our rather pallid, however rigid, Puritanism has developed in an era of expansion, considerably relieved of its poetry and, generally, in light marching order, Rousseauism has entered in triumph the citadel of our Philistinism. No doubt a frontal attack on this position would be quixotic, but if anything like an undermining transformation may intelligently be hoped for, it can hardly be that the spirit of style, considering its apt and manifold applicability, would fail to prove a promising agency. The æsthetic need of the "natural" man, and of the day in which he flourishes so generally and so luxuriantly as quite to dwarf by contrast the green bay-tree of the erstwhile wicked, is to have their energies, so vast and in many respects so beneficent, "shaped up." And to that end an ideal of style, running as it does through both life and art, and thus admirably calculated to compass precisely this result, is so much the primary as to be in effect a preliminary consideration in the practical æsthetic philosophy of each.

The first step, because the most fundamental, that it would take would undoubtedly be the displacement, so far as possible, of the cordial belief in the sacrosanct character of "naturalness" as a subjective manifestation natural in an egoistic age —plainly a herculean stride at the outset. But "naturalness" as such, however temperamental its sanctions, has certainly no immunity from critical analysis. And the first thing about it remarked by analysis is the distinction, often lost sight of, between the natural and the normal. The normal is quite the last thing our revolutionists deal in or, for that matter, believe in. Subtracting the poetry from Rousseauism, they worship nature only as will—one's own, of course. Abstractly they as well as everybody else would admit the normal to be the legitimate—or, if the word be suspect, the laudable—aim of all our activities. Abstractly, no one advocates the unnatural, any more than the abnormal. But concretely it is quite as apparent that the merit and value of naturalness depend on the nature expressed or exhibited in it, not on any nature's acting in accordance with its instinctive impulses, since it is so very perfectly possible for these impulses to prove deplorably abnormal. Even those "friends of man" to whom Doctor Watts extended the privilege of delighting to bark and bite because such is their nature, confer more, and perhaps experience no less, delight for being subjected to some restraint of these expressional energies. And a similar discipline in natural demeanor is effective as a civilizing agent in the social development of man himself.

Nor is the usefulness of social pressure of the kind limited to the primitive community, though the individual who is a group-leader in some circles would certainly be what is known as a "group-breaker" in others of higher differentiation on account merely of being himself insufficiently "broken in." Everyone has remarked the conjunction of the unknown face and the familiar manner noted by Mr. Herford. Of course coltishness in the colt is appropriately natural. Even so, it is much modified before he is ready for human society. But man's nature should, because it can, aspire higher—to be born again, for example, in various respects. Much of his conduct, his nature thus transformed, belongs in the æsthetic field and aptly responds to æsthetic sanctions. To justify it by those shared with the beasts of the field is to fail to do it justice. And in the modelling that life gives to the common clay of our common human nature some are carried much farther than the mere sketches it leaves of others. Logically, thus, the "naturalness" of those whose natures are developed exceeds in calibre and excels in quality that of those less transformed and, though farther from the normal, strictly speaking more natural—and obviously outstrips that of those remaining, after such imperfect metamorphosis as Bottom's "translation," like him, essentially unchanged. Nature crude and nature cultivated—whether by art or life—wear different masks. The main difference between them will be that due to the degree of perfection reached in the transmutation of instinct and impulse into character and control—an achievement certainly fostered by the introduction into their activities of the spirit of order and measure, and crowned by the interpenetration of rhythm, as pertinent, surely, to life as to art.

No doubt many remember, though apparently alas! must "remember as forgotten," the Victorian commonplace that simplicity and "naturalness" are far from being the same thing—in personal quality any more than in artistic expression. The heart of man, having long ago, as we know, been observed to be deceitful above all things, as well as desperately wicked, it follows that simplicity has long been noticed—by all but the simple, no doubt—to be a quality considerably complex and elusive, partaking in its essence of the "culture conquest." Simplicity of moral attitude is as charming as it is rare and doubtless as accidental as genius, but, æsthetically, patrician simplicity is apt to outshine plebeian. Those who know him speak oftener of the subtle than of the simple savage. Our metropolitan varieties, to be sure, are simpler—more absorbed, at any rate, in being simply savage. Since the diffusion of the kindergarten one must suppose the public at large—at least among us, where, as a character of Henry James discovered, the position of a child is one of great distinction—to have learned, what all parents must always have known, that the child merely as a child is a puzzle personified. And "all the men and women" upon the stage of "all the world" being "merely players," they must not merely learn their many parts, but if they are to play them in public must study even their entrances and exeunts, as players have to, in order to play them naturally, *i. e.*, normally.

The ordering of one's nature with a view to seeming natural by being normal, is a business demanding the tension involved in realizing an ideal, and decidedly not relaxation in the arms of instinct; otherwise art would not seem so long and life so short to the indubitable majority of us—however often nowadays Pegasus may appear the "soonest curried" of "short horses" and "modern art" make modern life at times seem superfluously long for savoring its satisfactions. So complicated, in a word, is his nature that the amount of pressure requisite to compress the exuberance of the "natural man" within the chaste confines of simplicity is dejecting. Means of grace, æsthetic and moral, need to be invoked, and self-control employed, to the end of wearing his nature's garments with apparent ease and real effectiveness. Invocation of such aids would doubtless seem superfluous and exercise of such restraint be irksome to those with whom self-expression merely means self-disclosure, and who set self-display before self-direction, fancying themselves the while gloriously unfettered, though appearing to the unsympathetic eye as merely unbuttoned. But it is an unwary exaltation that leads so many among us (relying on agreement with the numbers in which there is, in reality, quite as much peril as safety) to conceive as emancipation what may very well instead prove merely the condition consequent on having been set adrift by the Zeitgeist, continually detaching detritus on its constructive onward and upward way.

At all events, before replacing the ideal injunction, "Be ye therefore perfect, even as your Father which is in Heaven is perfect," by the more modern and less exacting "Be yourselves," it would undoubtedly be only prudent to consider whether one is of those, rather, to whom the assertion "Ye are of your father, the devil," was addressed. I do not myself hold that the present age is probably the "little season" for which this individual was to be "loosed," as prophesied in the Apocalypse, for the excellent reason, if for no other, that he does not appear to have served the thousand years of bondage prophesied as immediately preliminary to this period. But, on the other hand, it is difficult to accept the assertion so frequently made that the salient traits of today are merely those immemorially illustrated in the succession of youth to eld. The head and front of its uniquity consists in the fact that, instead of taking the torch to hand on to its successor, supplied with fresh fuel and all the latest improvements, the present age has apparently extinguished it—with ignominy or ignominiously, as one chooses—and fashioned a new one for itself, whether destined or even designed for transmission being exceptionally uncertain. It engages in the race of progress less as a true than as a biological "sport," one may say, if the pun be pardonable in the interest of its pertinence. And the quality of current wisdom in thus cutting loose is indicated by its selection of one of the most remarkable of historic periods as the one chiefly meriting a contempt but slightly alloyed with compassion—an attitude impossible to instructed reflection, and therefore, no doubt, attributable to group contagion. Yet, so widely has it popularized this attitude, it was almost startling to read recently in the liberal London *Nation*, which ought to know the group in question, that "no one whose opinion is worth stopping to listen to ever uses the word 'Victorian' as implying dulness, stupidity, or uninspired convention."

Arnold speaks of the "feeling of tightness and oppression" and "desire for clouds, storms, effusion, and relief" that, as the spirit of antiquity wore itself out, the world came to have. Who has not heard something of this sort expressed by exponents of the present day as produced in themselves by the last age? Even today there is much talk of "escape"—even from this age, from everything evidently but one's cherished self. The feeling and desire recorded by Arnold came to fruition in the thirteenth century and were incarnated in Francis and Giotto and Dante. The revulsion that inspired the revolt—centuries in incubating—sprang from the growing inefficacy of a dying civilization gradually developing into a different one long in culminating. One suspects the present age of having its tongue in its cheek a good deal, but certainly its humorists will hardly count on the credulity of those who remember Victorian days in asserting any particular analogy of its own revulsion and revolt to this august and age-long sequence of genuine cause and effect; and cause and effect functioning on the uplands instead of at the nadir of mankind's thought and feeling. Its Francis, Giotto, and Dante are yet to appear, and Victorian justification for feelings of tightness and oppression so acute as to operate on an entire generation with the celerity of a jail delivery is the kind of figment born of irresponsibility unchecked by information. Its revulsion and revolt and its consequent conversion wholesale to wholesale naturalism must be otherwise explained.

There is, to be sure, one signal respect in which naïvely the present day, unsuspicious of its sonship, appears very considerably the prolongation rather than the repudiation of its predecessor; and in fact in many things of the moment we may assuredly assay less novelty than resides in the degree to which they are pushed. No one would call the age an original one. Its *excess* certainly *is* novel. Since Aristotle's association of virtue with moderation, the elect have in general proscribed excess. But among the Victorians as early as the forties there were, for one notorious category, numerous specimens aptly catalogued under the classic vinculum, "short-haired women and long-haired men"; plenty of radicals who prized publicity above riches and to whom unobtrusiveness was either affected or abject, who preferred experiment to experience and deemed the proverbial out of date, whose thinking was an exercise of the fancy, whose feeling was febrile and mostly fleeting, who railed at regularity as dull and system as stupid, and who here and there developed a social phase known in the early seventies as "chromo-civilization." Gradually and insensibly they seem to have come in from the outskirts of social density to occupy the centre of the stage—never defended by us with much assiduity—and having, no doubt, during their swarming, as now recognized by the "orthodox" in the case of homœopathy and unitarianism, done much good on the way in modifying the rigidity of regularity. It may very well be, however, that before they are firmly established as the head of the corner they will be rejected of new builders and some refluent wave sweep them back as débris to the fringe of things. One should remember that there is a wonderful amount of formal education going on all the time. And anything may be prophesied of a period of pure flux—even its settling.

Still, "settling" takes time, and both the current record and recent history—especially day-before-yesterday's, notorious as the most completely forgotten—have more claims upon us than speculation about the future, for which, moreover, as Patrick Henry observed of the past in general, they constitute the only possible basis. The current record, copiously annotated and illustrated by the newspapers, reveals the spread of chromo-civilization in many quarters, its unrestrained "naturalism" actively stimulated by a lateral extension everywhere of articulateness outstripping art as larger and larger areas of individuals become more and more—and more thinly—educated. In the course of this transforming process less and less does the present day exhibit the measure and restraint, the order and movement of mind and manners that, permeating all ranks, mark an organic as distinguished from an anarchic civilization. It shows itself increasingly impatient of principles and prescriptions, and galled by every coercing direction of convention, the soundness of which it has no adequate equipment for perceiving.

Without fundamental study the *status quo* in whatever field tends rapidly to become the *status quo ante*. When challenged by ignorance of the philosophy of which it is a reasoned result, and the experience of which it is a tested survival, it is bound to seem outworn. The more smoothly it works the less it appeals to the enterprising but uninstructed imagination unaware of the friction it subjugates—the duller, in a word, it seems. Acquaintance with its *raison-d'être*, its various *raisons-d'être*, would often reconcile incipient revolt against it into resigned acceptance of its rule. It has been said, for instance, that if the South had read *The Federalist* it would not have seceded.

Furthermore, as in the field of art and letters style has become prosaic in consequence of being deemed conventional, and has been so deemed because it involves constructive and conforming effort in constraint of expansive impulse, so in the field of social and personal expression it has been coincidently submerged by inexperienced experimentation revelling in that order of functioning which, proceeding from impulse, is devoid of design. A logical corollary is its disposition to dispense with taste—always, in worth while differentiation, an acquisition, as presupposing knowledge.

"Taste?" exclaims a writer in the London *Mercury* in the course of an elaborate consideration of the subject: "Never mind about taste, so long as you can get *appetite*," a counsel of perfection connoting less the table than the trough, and not merely echoing the naturalistic philosophy of an undiscriminating age, but sounding an ominous premonition of "the morning after," when taste *is* a mockery and appetite mirage, and the dying penitent endeavoring to turn his thoughts heavenward is warned by his confessor to be thankful he has a hell to go to. Socially and personally, in fine, the current record shows us engaged in an attempt to perpetuate the carnival. Naturally, the philosopher and the historical student predict instead a long Lent with no Easter in view.

Supplementing the social picture thus sketchily suggested, day-before-yesterday's history accounts for it by reminding us that when our radical and adventurous element—tending by disposition toward the "larger liberty of the new freedom," chafing with a growing restiveness under restraints of which they had forgotten, or conceived they had outgrown, the sanctions, and feeling the undirected impulses due to the mere expansion of energy—perceived the immense increase in the alternative opportunity afforded and competitive pressure imposed by increasing wealth and population, this element had only to mark time to find its own ranks greatly increased also. By the same token, marking time was the last thing it thought of. Instead, it set out on its march. Soon, becoming conscious of itself *as* an element, it acquired the sense of power and the illusion of virtue which come from association with those who, in Cicero's phrase, think the same things concerning the republic. And these acquisitions enabled its spokesmen to make the business of propaganda practical, productive—and remunerative; though often, perhaps, in other respects than wealth; which did not so much matter, publicity being preferred. At the same time I remember hearing some years ago an eminent lawyer say that a man who in 1896 had $100,000 and ten years later was not rich could have had no business capacity. Those were the years when Social Unrest appeared and capitalized itself into permanence. There were so many people without the requisite $100,000 to start with! The national social unity, uniformity itself compared with that of Europe, began to show disintegration, subtly at first, then—even before the Great War came on—by very sensible stages, its crystalline structure, so to say, gradually dissolving in the flux which has since, becoming rapidly more and more dilute, widened into a flood, submerging old types and all standards, whirling to the surface whole strata of the "suppressed," ardently adventurous, full of confidence and courage and—above all—eager to discover and enjoy the *segreto per esser felici*.

So far, I imagine, everyone, spectator or participant, is agreed as to the character and origin of the spectacle affording this "dissolving view" of our society at large. But what has not, I think, been sufficiently remarked is the very considerable extension of the picture due to the entire emancipation of an entire sex. This accession has potentially, if not yet practically, doubled the numbers of our larger social as well as political public, and what social observer who has noted what it is that makes the world go round would deny that it has in a still greater degree modified its character? Woman, having changed her political status, or having had it changed for her, has inevitably transformed her social sphere by engaging increasingly in the activities of society at large instead of confining herself to those associated with "home and society." Her equivalence to man, always recognized by the reflecting, having received public consecration by legislative enactment of her new political equality with him, has received also, together with a new impetus, a new direction. Socially speaking, she was, even in the days of her "subjection," if a prisoner, also a jailer. She was the trusty who held the social keys. Having shaken off her own shackles in the spirit consonant with *her* new freedom, what wonder that her native chivalry led her to open the cell doors and liberate the sex which, in the interest of a now superseded state of things, she had kept so rigorously under lock and key, but with which—as now appears—she would all along have preferred to romp, fraternizing with it in the character of "a fine, clean boy" now become so generally her ideal. Hence complications with, as always, compensations, adequate or not, as time, which is said at last to make all things even, may decide. The social penal code is under radical revision, at all events, and it has for some time been plain that no longer divorce, but marriage itself, is, as it were, on trial. Recently, too, an eminent British novelist, taking a generally cheery view of the near future, prophesied for it an indefinite extension of the privileges of maidenhood as a suffrage result. But the British are notoriously more advanced than ourselves in these matters—as in theology.

Meantime, there is hardly one of the new features of the present-day social panorama that would not be ameliorated if modified by a general spirit of order that is organic and of movement that is rhythm—such simplicities as harmony in feeling and grace in conduct. The recognition of this spirit and inspiration by it should have no small share in any successful circumvention of the unsystematized moral and material conditions amid which we live. We do, however, very actively live. Those of our croakers who only croak should not forget so important a detail of the data pertinent to any consideration of present-day deficiencies. Manifestly the spirit of decorum, fundamental in any functioning of the spirit of style, enters a good deal into the matter as an essential, civilizing factor, and decorum as manifestly implies the discipline that is one of the fundamental antipathies of the haphazard and capricious spirit of "naturalness" now not only predominating in our practice but presiding among our ideals. The idea itself of discipline today evokes distaste. It involves constraint, and we chafe at constraint even more than we resent control, which merely curbs independence, whereas constraint compels conformity and therefore motivated instead of desultory activity. This, of course, means work, and few would maintain that a disposition to shoulder the burden originally imposed as a punishment for sin was as natural as the laziness that so largely manages to escape it. In the physical field our various necessities direct the energy developed by growth, but in the mental we are constrained to useful effort only, or mainly, by ideal disciplines. And logically we need disciplines as we need other desirable things in proportion to our lack of them.

From this point of view one of the most valuable uses of style considered as Mr. Sherman's formative pressure is its disciplinary use; and not in formal education only, but in the self-culture that has a claim to be conterminous with life. It is a familiar commonplace that education educes, but probably even in the hands of a follower of Socrates it educes less the contents than the capacities of the mind. If it is to instruct as well as develop, it must also induce a considerable increase of contents. To the contents, as at the outset they confront it, we may safely apply the remark of Thucydides regarding early Greek achievements applied by Arnold to Wordsworth's famous "Intimations," and opine that they are "no very great things." In any case they are chaos and undesirable to return to. The prophet warning of the wrath to come speaks instinctively of a return to chaos as the least desirable of pilgrimages. The return to nature in any other sense than that in which the snake sloughs his outworn skin is relapse—not the "release" complacently so called by our current Malvolian fatuity. The impulses to perfection detected in man's nature by Aristotle and Cicero remain inert until exercised, desultory unless developed. Also his nature harbors impulses to imperfection. Achievement, in proportion to its own importance, implies effort prolonged and painful. Swimming with the stream is hardly more voluntary and therefore little more "formative" than drifting with the tide.

Even if these indolent practices are more encouraged in formal education than in days when the curriculum was compulsory, imposing at the outset the directed diet otherwise inevitable at the other end of any satisfactory life, they are necessarily inhibited by self-culture—a process more familiar today in idea than in execution, perhaps, but at all events never anywhere, of course, carried far enough. In what may very well be considered one of its departments, the effect of the mind on the body, there is widespread interest today, and general effort to discover in this effect beneficent possibilities equivalent to its acknowledged evil ones. Meanwhile the effect of the mind on the mind is plainly not less real and perhaps as useful. Its agency in ameliorating conduct has been no secret for at least nineteen centuries—declared by Virgil and disclosed to Nicodemus, as doubtless anteriorly, and long before Hamlet's variant of the idea; and ever so little to "look within" is to be assured that in fact the action of the mind is largely determined by its attitude. It functions with least friction within lines of its own prescription. To practise anything with the constancy necessary for its perfecting it is not only helpful but needful first to get the idea of it clearly, definitely, firmly in mind and then make of this idea an ideal. Passivity wins no more victories than pacifism until its mere registry of protest against one ideal becomes active concentration upon another, its antithesis. One would be long in getting to the end of any road of which all the guide-posts warned instead of directing, or, indeed, if from the start one did not keep the end in mind until it came in sight. If, therefore, we invoke such simple æsthetic factors as order and rhythm and their organic synthesis to the end of emphasizing and aggrandizing the unity and, indeed, entity of whatever work the mind is concerned with, the product of mental process in whatever field of creation cannot fail to become more considerable than, being unconsidered, it could reasonably be expected to. The services of style to all our activities of art and life in contributing to them singleness, cogency, and charm tend in fact, as in logic, to become effective in proportion as the idea of style becomes one of our ideals. It is not an abstruse idea, nor is the idea of making it an ideal abstruse. Both are plain enough to ask without apology a share in the thoughts which find a harbor within the lowest brow that has room for any considerations of the kind. Of course any ideal must be certified by consciousness; the ideal of following impulse automatically either is not an ideal, or is superfluous, or is idiotic.

It is, as I have said, fantastic to attribute the present widespread surrender to impulse, the exuberance and excess by which it is marked and the philosopny with which it is defended to emancipation from oppression—more specifically and egoistically viewed as "suppression." Self-expressionists should in fairness reflect that in the matter of imperative suppression the alternative is sometimes either their impulses or themselves. In general our emancipated generation has at worst only had to follow the example of Artemus Ward's prisoner, who, after languishing for years in a dungeon, finally thought of opening the unlocked door and deserting the place. The joy of living was not altogether confined among the Victorians. They did not even allow the interest of others to lead them into wholesale prohibition of their own pleasures. No doubt society was more decorous, but one recalls times and occasions when sections of it failed of any very general attainment of its ideal in this regard. One would think indeed that its ideal was easily enough held and elastically enough administered to forestall the present revolt against, not the conduct it often failed to prevent, but the ideal itself, which the present day inseparably associates with hypocrisy, pluming itself on its own contrasting and, in its censors' view, shameless candor.

We may perhaps creditably dispense ourselves from rendering "the homage that vice pays to virtue," though to do so seems a little graceless. Certainly to expect vice to pay homage to virtue in an age bankrupt of homage in general would be sanguine. Elisée Réclus, in speaking of the English race, elaborates La Rochefoucauld's maxim by observing: "The number of hypocrites is, of course, most considerable where respect for personal dignity and love of truth are most held in honor." If therefore we are now celebrating a reduction in the number of our hypocrites, we ought to do so pensively and at least realize where we stand. Not too distant perhaps from where French society stood, awaiting the besom of the Revolution, when, as one of its many note-taking chiels remarked, virtue had been so much ridiculed that hypocrisy had disappeared. To accuse the age of honoring the love of truth less than its predecessor would seem surprising to it, and, indeed, the French geographer, naturally less exact than an epigrammatist, may have spoken loosely, throwing in his second trait for good measure. But there is no doubt about the diminution of personal dignity being a marked characteristic of our time, and in consequence it can be no affront to mention the fact. Assuredly no time was ever before so content with all its characteristics as to conceive the parade of its indecencies more laudable than their concealment. It is interesting to find this modification of self-respect, through the trituration of personality, in connection with the extravagant development of the individual which is equally to be noted, and which would manifestly be an anomaly if the particular individual developed in such profusion possessed personal dignity in proportion to his independence. But it should be remembered that his independence concerns his feelings and eminently not his thinking, which follows his feelings with docility and thus at the same time permits him more self-assertion without correspondingly increasing his self-respect.

The kind of independence that rewards surrender to nature has, in distinction from the freedom planned by design and achieved by effort, no tendency whatever to develop personality; rather the contrary. Merely emphasizing individuality, it does nothing to differentiate the nature of our quality from the quality of our nature, and the expression of personality, about which we hear so often as justifying so much, is what is perfectly known and understood as a self-assertion that asserts nothing about the self—except often its, in consequence, not particularly winsome existence. The order of personality quite generally developed by the age betrays, rather, its tendency to uniformity and its "natural" origin in the universal instinct of self-preservation—as its marked egoism, a direct and rather raw derivative of this instinct, also amply indicates. What the cultivation of style merely as an *objective* ideal might do to modify this decidedly dreary monotony should, so far as pertinence is concerned, be sufficiently obvious. "To be less and less *personal* in one's desires and workings is the great matter," declared Matthew Arnold, summing up his life's philosophy near its close. To take one's self for granted and, withdrawing one's attention from it as well as tempering one's tendency to "express" it to others, to concentrate one's mind on its development is, in the long run, to serve it best. The process, if successful, affords room also for quite a little arrogance—all, perhaps, that a hundred per cent American ought to allow himself. Nature makes the number of "selves" produced astonishingly close kin, and for the evolution of personality relies mainly on the man himself:

"Fool, if thou canst not pass her, rest her slave";

or—to include man in nature—relies on his own exercise of the faculties with which she provides him and his own constancy in pursuing the path of perfection. It is a rocky road all the same, and following it involves sacrifices and restraints. Personal dignity is, no doubt, restrictive of certain impulses, and it is entirely likely that it has been so largely discarded because of a general conviction that it, too, was a shackle; shackles of any sort, anything that can plausibly be called a shackle, even one, say, that keeps the moral centre of gravity from falling without the line of the base, having aroused widespread aversion. But I think that the cause of the phenomenon at once lies deeper and is, moreover, in this instance less specific than general in its effects—enough so, at all events, to warrant a more general consideration.

The spirit of the age, in many cases tired of the temple—in others driven from it this time *by* "them that sold doves"—instead of setting itself to transform the sanctuary, has fled to the forum, discarding the first of the fundamental commandments in favor of the second, "like unto," but by no means identical with it. It has thus abandoned the inner for the outer life, and if in consequence it has sagged into the practice and the philosophy of the natural man, adopting the gospel of "naturalness" in both life and art with an enthusiasm bordering on ferocity, it is not surprising that, as a natural corollary, it should have transformed the outer life itself. This transformation may be concisely described as a result of its determination to be henceforth not only in the world but of it.

Its ideal, therefore, is a radical revision of the opposite apostolic attitude, also hitherto, openly or secretly, consciously or unawares, that of the more elevated spirits among the idealists of the world; Keats, for instance, after characterizing mankind as "crowds of Shadows in the shape of men and women," declares: "The soul is a world of itself and has enough to do in its own home." Nevertheless such an ideal constitutes a complete answer to those critics of the age who charge it with lacking ideality altogether. More than that, it makes it a democratic age, an age in which democracy, already politically the working hypothesis of the world, has become also its social and personal ideal. Anyone who reflects must appreciate the great increase in the world's benevolence and beneficence, exercised in its industry, too, as well as inspired by its imagination along a far longer line than that from China to Peru, and rescuing from defeat as well as rewarding with success in the battle of life alike the beneficiary and the benefactor. The impressive catalogue alone of the "works" in this vast field, too voluminous for aught beyond passing allusion, may assuredly be credited in the ledger on the debit side of which figures unmistakably our well-known decline of "faith."

This decline dates from farther back than today

we are wont to realize. The bitterest censor of the Victorian age characterized it a half-century ago as "destitute of faith yet terrified at scepticism." Since then the "fifty years of Europe," supposedly superior to "a cycle of Cathay," have achieved the conquest of terror without, however, attempting the acquisition of faith. Such current variants of this virtue as are to be summed up in confidence that he who loveth his life the same shall save it illustrate but a perversion of Emerson's "Trust thyself," which it would never have occurred to the Sage of Concord nor to him of Chelsea to forestall. The words appended to the injunction—"Every heart vibrates to that iron string"—connote nothing epicurean or egoistic. "Soft Lydian airs" and the lute's "lascivious pleasing," on the one hand, and, on the other, the blare of the band-wagon are not farther from those vibrations than self-indulgence and self-assertion are from the self-reliance born of faith in the absolute and the eternal. Being of, as well as in, the world inevitably quickens one's sympathetic interest in it beyond the degree felt by the dweller in any ivory tower of detachment. Yet manifestly to become not only a partisan but a partner gives one a less objective view of it. Indeed, after becoming identified with it, and being already committed to the guidance of "naturalness," how take any but a worldly view of the world? Generosity evinced in acquiring this alliance is, naturally thus, a little modified after it is acquired. Self-interest, automatically producing partiality, instead of desiring to see itself as others see it, fancies others seeing it as it sees itself —that is, in the most favorable light possible. For an impartial view it is condemned to attend the slow processes of conscience and introspection. In the meantime to ask it, while still enchanted in the bonds of "naturalness" and still enthralled in its fusion with all around it, not to magnify what it regards itself as having gained, would be asking of it a diffidence it does not possess, not to say the kind of hypocrisy it professes to despise.

One thing is clear: pure laudation of the past never won any present from its ideals or its idols. It is obviously next to impossible even to describe the past in terms pleasing to the present. Ephraim undoubtedly breathed a sigh of relief when Israel was enjoined to "let him alone." In pursuing a different policy our conservatives probably do not quite appreciate, that for energy and efficiency, for the zest of life and the reward of effort, the one thing no epoch can afford to surrender, without becoming at best a silver age, is its initiative. Rather than pay such a price an age so abnormally heedless of the past as the present present would, one opines, prefer to be known as an age, not to say *the* age, of brass; though not, let us hope, the brass in which, as Shakespeare affirms, "men's evil manners live." Quite comprehensibly, too, however much better worth their attention others might find it if silver. In its conflict with "chaos and the dark" it must, above all things, as Emerson adjures us, "advance." If it have neither the wisdom to keep its bridges and ships unburnt in readiness for even purely strategic retreat and temporary recoil, nor the imagination needed, for instance, to conceive cookery apart from conflagration *à la chinoise*, it is doubtless none the less imperative that, even without a line of retreat or an adequate commissariat, it should advance, or deem itself advancing, until somehow and by something it is decisively pulled up. Not, let us trust, by disaster, though it would surely be more prudent if it could be persuaded to follow the example of the chambered nautilus and in building more stately mansions for its soul not insist on demolishing the existing edifice.

For among the contents of this structure there is manifestly to be found the collection of principles as well as phenomenal data that up to date the world has found useful. If the fittest survives it does not follow but it is not unlikely that a certain amount of fitness survives with it. Especially among the principles informing purely objective ideals the age might find some particularly adapted to its use in advantageously modifying its own—certainly those focussed in an element which enters so markedly into so many activities, spiritual and material, as the element of style. Some of these have been closely bound up in one way or another with the faith the decline of which is so general. And certain implications of this decline, with their traceable consequences, one must I think recognize as belonging among the disadvantages assigned us by the law of compensation; closer relations with His creatures are too dearly—as well as also too illogically—purchased by ceasing all relations with the Creator. Was that rather exclusive fundamentalist the Apostle James wiser than even he knew in declaring "friendship with the world" to be "enmity against God"? Or was he less wise than he thought when, after characterizing the practice of "visiting the fatherless and widows in their affliction" as "pure religion and undefiled," he charged its practitioners to keep themselves "unspotted from the world"?

Now of these implications, involved in the succession of the forum to the sanctuary, one is the paradox whereby the age, unstringing the bent bow of effort and lapsing into the intellectual languor of the "natural" man, relying the while for support on the dignity of human nature, nevertheless presents us with a typical individual man in whom egoistic expansiveness has considerably submerged the sense of personal dignity. Our whole conception of personal dignity, indeed, has suffered a strange if not rich sea change directly attributable, one would say, to the present-day development of the inner into the outer life, into the widespread determination I have emphasized to be of, as well as in, the world. Candor, for example, has usually hitherto been associated with innocence rather than sophistication (in either the traditional or the current sense of the word), so that we may speak of present-day candor, the candor that so smugly replaces Victorian smugness, as the new candor. It may at least be credited with self-possession, being a stranger to the blushes of confusion and the attitude of apology. But self-possession does not imply personal dignity as we used to know it, and in fact we may speak of the new dignity as of the new candor. Reticence, formerly of its essence, would now seem pose. Publicity, once instinctively shunned, and if incurred winced at, is welcomed if not solicited, even publicity of privacies.

Sometimes mere private citizens, if the term is still appropriate, are—one can hardly say as unconscious but—as unblushing as actors; often, in fact, suggesting actors not acting, possibly out of deference to the new sincerity. Like the actor's, their personality is minimized at the same time that it is obtruded. Self-centredness seeks the centre of the stage on any terms—even disapproval of its acting. In certain presences one is reminded of the prime minister who replied to a friend urging his son for office and mentioning his modesty as a recommendation: "Modesty! What has he done to be modest about?" The personal note seems pressed even in the absence of all pretension.

On the other hand, wherever possible in the circumstances, nothing restricts the parade of pretensions. Save here and there one, the newspapers have considerably ceased to be anonymous, and the loss of the paper's authority as an institution, which used sometimes to be very great, a coördinating and stabilizing force in instructing and influencing public opinion, is not counterbalanced by any authority in the writers, who, save the impressionist "columnists," are often unknown. As, by the way, are half the signing reviewers of even standard books by writers of distinction. In circumstances permitting defiance, though hitherto prescribing observance, of decorum—such as those of the ballroom and the bathing beach—the new personal dignity shows itself perhaps at its farthest remove from the old. Here the competition in the expression of personality so dear to the age yields to the expression of the person. Possibly all these phenomena are matters of convention, and in time even the stickler for decorum will grow callous through familiarity with its absence. It is true that where nothing else is missed, conservatives may miss an outworn coquetry and balk at enduring, to say nothing of embracing, what needs but to be seen. But the philosopher will have his doubts about the entire cycle of new conventions of this order. As Arnold's Arminius, who advised the English of a half-century ago to "get Geist," he may reasonably, I think, counsel the generation committed to the heterogeneity of so much current "natural" and personal expression at least to reduce it to more coördinate order and more agreeable measure, and with these in view to "study style." Indeed mere reaction and pure fatigue may lead the more extravagant of our new dignity addicts to echo the more rudimentary need expressed by the sensible but shivering oyster of Mr. Don Marquis's wonderful poem, in its agonizing appeal, "Gimme clothes, gimme clothes!"

To be sure, Teufelsdröckh himself, though "not an Adamite," could not object to modification of the dross of outward garb in the interest of extracting the starch and removing the friction from social intercourse. And if the new dignity secured this result, or even aimed at it, even the fastidious would to that extent view it with favor. It is, however, innocent of any such stylistic intention, being intrinsically egoistic rather than social and originating, perhaps, in a desire to experience a sensation by producing one—nowadays, owing to the business having been overdone, doubtless often a delusion. Sensation, at all events, in moral appetence as well as in social practice and bodily costume, is incontestably the order of the day. The time is positively thrall to it. In his preface to the "Twice-Told Tales," Hawthorne half apologized for offering his reader sentiment instead of passion. Today sensation has largely supplanted both. Sin having so generally disappeared from the contemporary conscience or consciousness (now, as with the Latin peoples, who have but one word for the two, pretty much the same thing with us), passion has perhaps perforce taken refuge in crime—abundant enough, to be sure, in what Mr. Philip Kerr aptly calls our "queer mixture of humanity and violence." Even vice has in some degree evaporated. Certain personal principles and social practices from which society used to be in part protected by the hypocrisy which we are told and indeed observe no longer exists, widely embraced in spite of their mien, have ceased to be widely accounted vicious through the mere process of acceptance and diffusion. The confines of fastidiousness have signally shrunk, pressed back, in some quarters at least, by what would once have been quite generally esteemed *canaillerie*. It may very well be that freedom, "fresh air," and familiarity will ultimately clarify the closer atmosphere of conservatory conventions, once unconsciously observed, but now too generally (in whose interest? one wonders) decried as prudish and prurient, to have preserved their old protective virtue. Indulgence in the illusions of hope was long ago proclaimed instinctive in man, and we see the future in great part through our temperaments. In this way we may take any view of it at the present time, being admittedly in a period of transition. For the moment, however, to use an unimpeachably up-to-date barbarism, passion may be regarded as "debunked." And sentiment has been treated still more drastically. Sentiment, in fact, as a general social and personal factor, has not survived the ridicule of being called sentimental. It does lack an adjective, it is true, but why assign to it that belonging to sentimentality, except by way of expressly asserting that sentiment is sentimental—the common belief, of course; in fact a prominent article of the common creed? Yet the intellectual sanctions of a creed without sentiment need to be further developed, more universally familiar, and more constantly kept in mind if they are to serve as effective protection against evils hitherto avoided through the agency rather of the soul than the mind. Few reflective observers in modern days can have failed to have their attention sharply called to the relation of the decline of sentiment to perversions of the mind itself. Crime of the passionless is more disquieting, even if rarer, than the passionate variety, and there are minds that take seriously the current frivolity of deeming sentiment humbug.

The age is certainly juvenile enough to lose its schoolboy courage when it comes to confessing the particular weakness of sentimentality, but its juvenility is terribly complicated by jejuneness, so far as sentiment is concerned, in what it calls —at every possible opportunity—"sex." The term "sex" it probably regards as a euphemistic triumph, and except in the field of art it is almost its sole abstraction, though, one judges, not the least of its preoccupations. Indeed, how to turn it into the concrete must give constant concern not to its pure, but to its practical, imagination—to borrow the Kantian distinction. As Henry James said, apropos of Maupassant, one thinks about it a good deal when one thinks of nothing else—approximately the condition to which some of our prominent fictionists study to conform. This one might think not wholly unfavorable to sentiment—if only as a by-product—but the dangers of the situation, however insidious, are obviated by the grossness of determining the interest to sensation instead. The reign of sensation, on the other hand, was from the first implicit in the abandonment of the inner life for the outer, and this abandonment in turn has been involved in being of the world so completely as to deprecate any degree of detachment from it. Even emotion, exteriorized sufficiently, is subtly transformed into sensation—even when it is inspired by the humanity justly noted by Mr. Kerr. It gets early outside the mind's control, and from instinctive sympathy easily develops as automatic appetite. Emotion ceases to be a force, like sentiment, and becomes the weakness inherent in a craving. The susceptibility is supplanted by the sense and the intellect by the nervous system. Emotion of one kind or another, and as contrasting with reflection, is all the same—is all the more—characteristic of the present day, and the service that may be rendered by the spirit of style to coherent and convincing expression of it is obvious. Plainly such service is not likely through affinity to attract an age so avid of sensation as to be suspicious of sentiment, but as plainly to such an age it would for that reason be all the more likely to prove salutary, and may therefore pertinently be signalized as useful.

VI

PRESENT-DAY USES—ART AND LETTERS

Subordination to sensation of both sentiment and style is not peculiar to ourselves but general, no doubt, in the modern phase of art and taste. In Paris, where one would think style inveterately established, and even in quarters there where it was most salient, it has quite notoriously and riotously taken, as it were, a holiday. This, longer apparent in plastic art, is now also shown in the drama, which, as regards style, furnishes "the acid test" in both art and the life it mirrors. One hears, for instance, that they now rant at the Français; indeed one divined it here a year or two ago; and it is easy to recall days when excess on the stage there produced murmurs of "*Charge!*" and subdued but heartfelt ejaculations of "*Non! non!*" in the house. Curiously enough, Mr. Norman Trevor, the actor, recently back from an English visit, is reported as saying of the English stage: "It has deteriorated in respect to both plays and acting. There is an overzealous attempt to be natural, resulting in underacting, and a great deal of apathy all around." *Multum in parvo* surely in its bearing on the relation of "naturalness" to style. I remember Sarcey occasionally holding the actor up to his art in the same way, notably Fèbvre, too, whose underacting was decidedly *stylé*. In Paris, however, the tendency to revert to routine is, in general, in the direction of style. Our own tendency is away from it. In the matter of style French infidelity is due to stimuli of a transitory nature; with us, as no doubt with the English, whose traits and tradition we, naturally, so largely share, coldness to it comes rather from fatigue in the struggle to hold an unfamiliar pose. The "natural" in one case pulls toward style and away from it in the other. We associate distinction with reserve, the French with development. We have an instinctive partiality for storing energy, they for using it; we prefer the sense of power, they the functioning of force; while therefore we are always affirming character, they are constantly exercising mind, and (like the Greeks) incline to the architecture, as we (with the Romans, rather) to the engineering, of expression.

Our distrustful feeling toward style thus proceeds in part, no doubt, from a natural bias in favor of the restricted order of beauty proper to a Quakerish taste—such as, for a striking example, is attested on a large scale by the æsthetic aspect unifying the city of Philadelphia, still the pride in this respect of its founders' descendants, among whom our social standard is, perhaps, highest. And the hostility to style into which at the present time our distrust has apparently deepened, is, I suspect, to some extent reinforced by the drab and spare strain in our conception of refinement. This view, through regarding art as artificial and associating something Babylonish with beauty, results in imaginative poverty and the absence of æsthetic standards in the inescapable circumstances that imperatively call for them; Penn at court cut but a poor figure before Charles uncovering in his stead. And such æsthetic asceticism tends automatically to accentuate the ideal of "naturalness" that has possessed itself of the various fields of our thought, feeling, and conduct, and—to use the kind of style to which we are not hostile—lock, stock, and barrel.

Certainly the field of art and letters is as conspicuously controlled by this ideal at the present time as that of personal and social activity, and accordingly is as plainly ruled by the sensationalism implicit in a naturalistic philosophy culminating in a cult of heterodoxy and a heterogeneous practice. Despite exceptions of note everywhere, despite a noteworthy general capacity (as if that were enough!) exhibited in writing as writing, and despite a technical level in many cases higher than often reached hitherto (the number of practitioners having enormously increased), the average novel must succeed in being "gripping," the average fine-art exhibition something with more "snap" than the merely admirable, the average essay "vital" or "devastating," the average poem "dynamic," the average play "thrilling." There is an occasional flaw showing a momentary shift but no steady breeze in the direction of reaction. One of the most pungent of present-day critics recently complained of our prize performance in letters, the short story, that it had sacrificed philosophy to "punch" and delivered its punch with mechanical rigidity—a blazing indiscretion from the popular point of view and one calculated to cheer the conservative with the rosy prospect if not of the revival of philosophy in the short story at least of the decline of punch. But the agencies interested in prolonging its present "rubber-stamp" rigidity are discouragingly numerous. They do, to be sure, conspire to give one a sympathetic comprehension of the current attitude toward Victorian rigidities. If, as the French adage has it, one is never so well scratched as by one's self, one is never so easily rasped as by others. Remembering this, all that

Victorian survivals could justly say to their censors in extenuation of their own varieties of commonplace would be, "Strike, but read me." Perhaps, too, that would be an unreasonable request to make of writers who, doubtless in self-protection, read only each other—with the retributive result, however, of belittling Howells, say, while extolling Mr. Dreiser. Probably Mr. Dreiser provides more thrills.

Thrills clearly are among the dearest desiderata of the day, despite their tendency to undermine tone and leave the victim not, to be sure, Hamlet's "passion's slave," but as surely a passive instrument to be played upon as "upon this pipe." Sensation itself thus appears distinctly limited sensuously. Its upper reaches, "calm and free," where the elevated and the exquisite wait to be experienced are left much unvisited. The test of it is thrill. Thc general public would quite generally echo the succinct formula used by a representative "girl of the period" in telling a remonstrant mother "where to get off": "If a thing isn't a thrill it's a bore." And the test of thrill is intensity; that of intensity being all you can stand. Critical "reactions" of this kind, accordingly, correspond in value to those of the hysterical child touching a hot stove with tentative finger. The contented sigh of the Paris bourgeois, as he settles himself into his seat at the Français of a Sunday afternoon, expectant of the pleasure to be derived from the *beaux vers* of the repertory, breathes a different order of beatitude.

Our stage may avoid such rant as there may be at the Français, declamation not being in any case its strong point, but the stampede of our theatregoers by the Russian agonists furnishes striking evidence of our preference for being played upon to being played to. Russians themselves, so vividly depicted in Mr. Gherardi's so happily entitled fiction, "Futility," would doubtless quite generally have echoed the sentiments of the member of this company who, taken by an American actor to an American theatrical performance, and invited to give his impressions, replied unenterprisingly that he found the attempt to get any futile, as he didn't understand what was said on the stage. When, however, without understanding what is said on the stage one can hear it from the street, a new element is introduced. The performance ceases to be pure pantomime, which stimulates in composure the spectator's imagination, and becomes pantomime plus the noise which, disconcerting receptivity, can only hypnotize the sensibility. The noise, combined with some of the drama and much of the action, produced a curious effect, delight or dismay according to taste, but certainly chiefly sensational. Meantime, the admirable art of the players, if conspicuous enough to "ride the whirlwind and direct the storm" in a way which the elect could savor, could hardly by itself have "thrilled" the general. Even the elect demand more stimulant at the theatre than formerly. A successor of Winter and Wheeler and Dithmar, dramatic critics of olden times, who wrote about the play and its performance, finds the greatest merit of an otherwise almost wholly charming play to have been the success of the heroine in filling him with real fear that she would succeed, in spite of restraint by a couple of other actors, in throwing herself out of a window, and producing in him, accordingly, delicious sensations —which must be indifferent to the reader.

The violence that Mr. Kerr couples with our humanity is observably infiltrating our taste in many directions. It is curious to see it associated so amicably with the featureless placidity of our excellent newspaper writing. Banished from the style, it riots in the substance, of this, sometimes paying lavishly for the privilege. The best newspaper talent we have records a prize fight in Wyoming, to do which, obviously, it is necessary to go there. Substance the most extravagant in the way of opinion and emotion, informs statement of the utmost composure. Ships were never scuttled in a milder manner. Confronted with what calls for concentrated effort, even energy quails, side-stepping ordered emphasis. Impudence itself is clearly too inadvertent and absurdity apparently too genuine to be effectively presented. Paradoxes are innocently proclaimed in the amiable but unwitting guise of platitudes. The tawdriest thinking clothes itself in the plainest garb, and what is so happily called "piffle" pleads for a hearing on the ground that prattle is not pretentious. In such unquestionable shape does the reincarnated ghost of Victorian "smugness" walk. Fundamental good nature is everywhere regnant. Self-satisfaction produces it in abundance, and we have thus found a way of all being very kind, and also in many cases very brutal at the same time. Universal tolerance prevails, according perfectly with complacence. The complacence is sometimes colossal. "We shall let slip by in charitable silence the centenary of George Eliot," observed the editor of one of the Literary Supplements on that occasion; a remark that Arnold, who divided the stylistic savagery of his time between "freaks" and "violences," would probably have catalogued under both heads. One visualizes the genial author of it revolting from Victorian "tightness and oppression," and, amid the "storms, clouds, effusion, and relief" of a freer age, tapping it out on his typewriter almost absent-mindedly. There is no vitriol in the contempt expressed for dignitaries felt to be "has-beens," and incapable of further harm; as Fields in one of their skits used to say to Weber, who complained of neglect: "You don't look neglected, you look forgotten."

But their successors, after crowding them off the board, yet await the ordeal prescribed by *Punch's* Milesian drill-sergeant: "Prisint arrms! Heavens, what a prisint! Step out here and look at yourselves!" And if in the contempt of these for their predecessors there is no acerbity, neither is there any moderation; excess has become fairly instinctive and impulse despotic. "So long as no bones are broken," one almost hears the literary exponent of the Zeitgeist's present temper exclaim, "the wincing of the weakling and the aversion of the dilettante *are* negligible. The bloom of life may take care of itself as it can. Manner, after all, merely veils matter, which alone has meaning. We are after the fruit, not the flower. Let us say so with manly candor, leave off playing tin soldiers with the elegances of expression, and recommend to those who still affect them the mandolin instead." Indeed I borrow this last injunction from one of the most authoritative, shall I say? at any rate most engaging, voices among the newspaper daily prophets—so different from those that discharged the same function among the Hebrews. Even those that persecuted Saint Paul for a particularly fine quality of what—including far inferior grades—we now call "liberalism," would stare at the charge of a recent "columnist" of distinction that this apostle was guilty of "taking the fun out of Christianity"—an assertion containing, as Voltaire said of the title Holy Roman Empire, three mistakes, and recalling the criticism of an eminent writer's use of a large "M" for Mahometanism, and a small "c" for Christianity as "an apparent attempt to contravene the judgment of ages betraying an imperfect conception of the relation of means to ends." The motive, or whim, of this rather conspicuous aside of "current comment" appeared, however, more clearly in the sequence, explaining that what was particularly exasperating in Saint Paul's offense was its "ineptitude," adding that Judas at least got paid, and betraying in its excess, one would say, the desire both to give and in giving to receive a sensation of an unusually acute order. Sensation, no doubt, acquires an extra edge through the perversion of uttering an enormity as a commonplace, but the point beyond which the sensational becomes the shocking is difficult to determine, and it can hardly be maintained that the shocking would lose even half its grossness even in losing all its evil. And of course the skin that is constantly subjected to it gets thicker and thicker as time goes on, "Nature" protecting herself admirably when it is a question of developing callus, however little in less material matters she may do for *us*.

The vice of sensation giving and seeking from an æsthetic point of view is that nothing can be made out of such an unmapped country as sensationalism. It is the home, or habitat, of pure whim. In the domain of the fantastic one thing is as good as another, because all are meaningless. The sensation which has succeeded to the Victorian sentiment, so mechanically nowadays reproached with conventionality, is all too incapable of conventionalization, having no pattern nor the potentiality of any. The character of a cause is negligible when only effect, any effect, is desired. Drugs do not interest laic analysis. Of course the desultory is distraction, and there are times when what Emerson called the almanac style is exceptionally diverting and newspaper flotsam suits us better than the "values" of literature, or for that matter of life. But, having these latter values in mind, one concludes that sensation will have to become, as Daisy Ashford would say, "less mere" before it can be utilized as either inspiration or material of the importance possessed by sentiment. It calls for the discipline of measure and restraint in any case, and concentration through style upon its effect may be commended to it, since effect, indeed, is its goal. It is irrational that the present day should not perceive the advantage of systematizing the expression of its emotional exuberance through the application of such a universal principle and the agency of such a universal language as style furnishes for just its need—its dire need—of lodgment in any mind it may desire to impress.

And whatever his success with the public, filing his own sensibility to an extra edge, instead of exercising it in ordering and animating its artistic material, is plainly perilous to the moral balance of the artist in proportion to the degree of acuity reached. Intensity of gaze—also a trait peculiar to the "modern" artist—may easily be carried so far as to induce neglect of what is outside of its focus, but that is a trifling handicap beside the concomitant excitation of nerves and emotions whereby the pursuit of sensation irritates and enfeebles the whole nature and hamstrings constructive effort. Control and composure and subjection of whims to principles produce solider as well as more agreeable results. Besides, to communicate "thrills" it is not enough to feel them.

"Dear laws, be wings to me,"

prayed Alice Meynell to the laws "of verse" which, if they did not "in the highest empyrean have their birth," were yet eminently not begotten of the present lawless generation of "mortal men." And Mr. Yeats, whose interest in style I have already illustrated, has a reference to that tragic figure, John Davidson, which vividly, if indirectly, characterizes the futility of much present-day sensational extravagance, content to "express itself," though expressing little else, casually rather than in style of any characterizable sort, serried or spacious, stately or severe. "With enough passion," he says of Davidson, "to make a great poet, through meeting no man of culture in early life he lacked intellectual receptivity, and, anarchic and indefinite, lacked pose and gesture, and now no verse of his clings to my memory."

Nothing could be more succinctly suggestive of the value of cultivating style than this truly sapient sentence. And poets, with or without enough passion to be great—a preliminary qualification perhaps unreasonable to exact of a prosaic period —as well as our numerous writers in all kinds who, in lieu of eschewing, incline to cultivate, the "anarchic and indefinite," should realize what therein they sacrifice. If, on the other hand, they have the receptivity which the age's profession of open-mindedness would argue general—except as regards the worth of its own inheritance, which it has so largely declined unexamined—they should recognize the value of "pose and gesture," frankly studied, if only to make "naturalness" seem natural. Even the natural bent for "a kind of felicity," admitted by Bacon in the idealization of nature, and such as delights us now and then in quite elementary cases—a native talent for pose and gesture comparable, say, to an exceptional singing voice—is none the worse for development. And this is how the matter should be looked at rather than, as is usual, the other way around of considering only the impossibility of developing such a gift without the germ to start with. Shakespeare, whose "most distinguishing characteristic," according to Carlyle, was "superiority of intellect," would doubtless more than another have smiled assent to the line in Ben Jonson's tribute declaring:

"For a good poet's made, as well as born."

And Mr. Max Eastman, an expert in these matters, as well as an authority on the sense of humor, having written a book about it, suggests the ingenious compromise: "An artist must train himself up to his own level." But, as I happened to read recently in M. Landormy's "History of Music," Bach did even better by "all his life long" copying and recopying the works of the masters, "and," says the author, "as a result of paying respectful homage to their knowledge, raised himself above their level"—a slow and tedious process, however, to commend to a generation satisfied with the simple and much speedier expedient of deeming its forerunners' level lower than its own. Professor Brander Matthews's essay inculcating "The Duty of Imitation" contains many instances of successful results from the persistent discharge of that obligation, but none more remarkable than this effect of impregnation by indirectness, which doubtless has much to say for itself, though it certainly had good luck in being taken up by Bach. The training of the subconsciousness, whereby habit becomes a second nature, is beyond question a practical discipline; Delacroix copied as protractedly and profitably as Bach can have done, and reading, rightly chosen and steadily pursued even if not studied, as well as increasing one's store of acquisition must have a suggestive influence upon his style.

But undoubtedly one's own powers must fundamentally be developed by themselves in active consciousness, with whatsoever guidance by suggestion or exercise in imitation. And in the matter of pose and gesture, where nevertheless artificiality is the arch-enemy, even the effect of spontaneity, surely the trump card of "naturalness," can only be secured by study. The converse of Sheridan's remark about easy writing being hard reading may, in many cases, be less exact than the remark itself, but in so far as easy reading demands seeming spontaneity, it requires either studied writing or extraordinary good fortune. It is, perhaps, not less difficult, and certainly more fundamental, to clarify than to color what one writes, but to achieve style by accomplishing both and, through the art that conceals art, endue the result with the effect of spontaneity, is harder still. Writers who learn how to do it in their sleep are few—though famous. The secret of the successful who do not is doubtless that, when the centre of the target is hit, hitting it seems to the observer easier than missing the target altogether. Vicissitudes of trial and error, the method doubtless assigned to man when the earning of his bread and its laboriousness originally became his destiny, are not visualized by the onlooker. The normal—or whatever our intelligence takes for it—is our only standard; consciously or unconsciously, we can have no other. Where we deem it attained we unconsciously assume it to have been reached by the direct normal route. Experience, that seasoned traveller, knows better—knows how often one has to stumble in, or stray from, the straight and narrow way, and, entering beckoning by-paths, to find oneself in Doubting Castle and the clutches of Giant Despair (and eke his dread consort, Diffidence!) ere reaching at last the Celestial City.

One of the most useful services that the cultivation of style could render the present day, and one quite within its competence as the friend of both parties, would be to mitigate the quarrel between the followers, respectively, of character and of beauty, which if not a standing is a smouldering one and is just now particularly active in both letters and art—the terms "life" and "art" having, for the moment, in the literary field, displaced the old ones. Mr. Middleton Murry, an authority in these matters whom I have already cited, speaking for a coterie of importance, one judges, represents the cleavage as having, in London, reached an acute stage in which he and his friends take the side of "life," deserting the banner of "art" in a notably whole-souled way. There is normally, no doubt, some such temperamental relation, not inconsistent with occasional coolness, between the two as that between love and duty prevalent in the Victorian era, sympathetically celebrated by the Victorian laureate, and now, perhaps, having been settled on naturalistic principles, no longer of interest. We already know of the present-day value set upon "life," the breezy view taken of it as a great improvement on conduct, its satisfaction in circumstances in which it can, as it were, pinch itself and realize that "this is the life." Art among ourselves is thought to wear, at times, an abandoned aspect—as who should say of Ariadne deserted by Theseus yet unconsoled by Bacchus. And possibly the kind of life that, to some extent, in her stead has found favor in our sight may, at times, have found so much less in hers as to lead her on her side to sulk a little. Yet the lifelong tie between art and life will probably not be permanently disrupted by an absolute divorce, even in the domain of fiction, in which they are certainly at present in many cases on abnormally frigid terms. Fiction is, doubtless, the field Mr. Murry has in mind—no one apparently, so far as current letters is concerned, having any other there, hardly even the poetry which, though its practice is so popular, singularly eludes mental retention. It seems only yesterday that, in England especially, both critics and practitioners of fiction were particular to refer to it as an art, sometimes in the tone of intimating that it was the only live one, as indeed its astonishing preponderance makes it seem. Mr. Percy Lubbock has certainly also demonstrated that it includes a prodigious degree of craftsmanship. On reflection perhaps that supplies one motive for purging it of art in favor of "life." A craft connotes apprenticeship—often so tedious even to talent and viewed by the ungifted with especial misgiving.

Nevertheless the normal relations between life and art may easily have been less fundamentally disturbed than the neighbors, as I suppose "the critics" may in this instance be called, have been inclined to believe. Invasion of the precincts of art by much of the life hitherto successfully kept out of them has, undoubtedly, created some scandal, but nothing so serious as the open-armed welcome it has received from the critics would lead one to suppose, and the situation may yet prove quite temporary. The normal relation between life and art may conveniently be called the intimate and inveterate one belonging to the marriage of material with meaning. Art may permissibly now and then take a holiday from interpreting and revel as efflorescence, but life can never cease to be potential artistic material. If it ever excusably seems meaningless, then for art that is its meaning—meaning on which it is less pleasant than profitable to reflect, and which for that reason perhaps is so often banished from the modern bosom, already actively predisposed to take unto itself the uninterpreted raw material instead. But the exile of art from that haven would not irreparably impeach its claims to unseverable fellowship with its legitimate substance, any more than a similar ejection would those of philosophy. "Like it or not"—as Stevenson would say—art will always arrange and animate, as philosophy will always examine and explain, the data furnished them by life. It is true that life is a larger thing than art, and that it has features which, practically considered, art may better interpret by imaging and illustrating in their own spirit of irregularity and of haphazard than by a more perfect foreshortened synthesis. It is only in theory that the microcosm can always focus the macrocosm into an adequate interpretative parallel. But this is plainly a matter not of art or no art, but of different technical methods. Each was very markedly employed by Thackeray, for instance. One may take his choice between "Esmond" and the others of the quadrilateral, as Taine did, rejecting all but "Esmond" as satire; as if, for that matter, satire were not art. But one had better choose both.

The effectiveness of the looser method appeared strikingly for the time being in the fiction of early French naturalism. At first the garishness of Zola's early books seemed to light up phases of life, as Thackeray said Fielding did a rogue, "like the flash of a policeman's lantern," and with such piercing vividness, seemingly secured by extended parallel presentation rather than the customary focussing of selection, as to produce the illusion that art had fled. Beauty was so plainly absent that one failed to note the companion theretofore so constantly in her company. The illusion was deepened by the flagrant novelty of encountering in an art form exactly and exclusively this kind of material—this order of "life." But "custom and use"—aided, one should always acknowledge, by Jules Lemaitre—later disclosed the fact that the fugitive was life rather than art. The reader has since had a surfeit of naturalism as a substitute for reality. Perhaps it was its inner unsatisfactoriness that led Zola himself to end one of his later books with unwonted eloquence and feeling: "*Tout n'est que rêve!*" Of course reality has to pass through the menstruum of the artist's mind, however little alembicated in the process. Having just read those masterpieces of our own fiction, "The Landlord of the Lion's Head" and "The Son of Royal Langbrith," I remember remarking, on some occasion of meeting their author, that his earlier books, though more romantic, seemed to me quite as real. "True," assented Mr. Howells; "only, when you are young life seems more like a fairy story to you." And "seems" must suffice us. Nobody really knows how it really is. But, outside the fairy-story field, it ought really to seem "as represented."

If, on the other hand, either the "epic" exaggeration or the cataloguing reproduction by art of the commonplace, the inconsequence, and the incoherence of life, or the dilettante artistry essentially detached from life, is what Mr. Murry bases his aversion upon, it is quite possible to "feel what he means." Even so, however, to express his meaning by a radical renouncement of art in general is to darken counsel. To encourage style would be far more salutary than to renounce art. And, indeed, I have dwelt so long on this characteristically contemporary blanketing of art by "life," and on the naturalism rather tardily but systematically modifying the realism of our own fiction, because it is precisely and obviously style, with its continuity and coherence that, permeating technical treatment, both topical and textual, should lift this fiction on the whole to a higher plane, viewed either as craftsmanship or as art. If we are not to have these agreeable qualities and their kindred as attributes of concrete substance in fiction, we shall be grateful for the pleasure they afford us, as abstractions, in arranging the pattern of the action, the position of the pieces, and the interplay of their relations, not to speak of the textual beauty of the libretto. There is certainly life enough and of enough pungency in the fiction of Maupassant, for an egregious instance, to show the compatibility of the worst of life with the best of art—the acme of art as art, in fact, and art too of which the central element is style.

It is, then, surely needless to abandon art out of loyalty to life, even the "life" by which—as so often happens with us since we selected for adoption that particular strain in French fiction, and whenever the word is used with unction—mainly misbehavior is meant. Indeed in this case art is particularly needful to fiction—at least, in the long run. "There comes a time, no doubt," Mr. Lubbock rather unaccountably makes a foolish character wisely say, in his delightful "Roman Pictures," "when we turn to life itself, to the book of the heart, rather than to an imaginary picture of it, however sincere; a mere novel then loses its hold on us, and we reach out after our kind." The requirements, in other words, are twofold: the novel must be something more than sincere as portraiture, and something more than "mere"—art, that is, as well as life. But the words quoted may be taken to imply the deeper meaning that we incline most to turn from art to life when art is heartless—something different, I imagine, from what Mr. Murry means. When it is not heartless (and not "mere") it is itself "the book of the heart," and, at need, a comforting equivalent for "our kind." And when is it not heartless? When it has itself at heart "the dim beauty at the heart of things." And when it has, it is able not only to "hold" us, but to hold us on the highest plane through the signal instrumentality of style enlisted in the sympathetic service of this beauty. It was not for nothing that the powers who preside over the destinies of literature, among the multifarious points of view of the Great Tragedy so multitudinously treated in fiction, should have reserved "the soul of the war" for the author of "A Son at the Front"—a title of happy equivalence to this its true theme—and the writer most distinguished among our contemporary fictionists for achieving beauty through style.

Today one can hardly use the word beauty without feeling a little self-conscious. One needs the courage of chivalry in the face of cynicism—it has so few friends. What indeed it is so often arrogantly conceived to suggest—the insipid, the inane, the superficial—deserves so few. Most phases of modern plastic, even more decidedly than literary, art take toward beauty a frankly supercilious attitude, viewing it at best as antiquatedly irrelevant—as much in the same case with its ancient copartners, goodness and truth, all three rather flat and fetichistic. Nature, too, is no longer, as heretofore understood, an inspiration but a realm in which to "peep and botanize," to find "volume" and "significant form." Having ceased to entertain sentiment in the soul, the modern movement has sought the development of "sensibility" as a substitute, but plainly a sensibility whose satisfactions must be largely "personal," since it so often confines itself to depicting nature as no doubt it can be seen but is not looked at. Its customary aspect is sacrificed to abstractions, and in two main directions. In one the artist endeavors by persevering concentration to capture the treeness of the tree, say, the skyness of the sky, the particularity of the particular place, the individuality of the individual—physically, of course, as a model and, it is to be understood in his interest, with but incidental, if any, reference to his moral personality. In the other, and at the opposite pole of intention, the artist uses the figure freely to depict (or, more strictly, licentiously to symbolize!) something invisible and immaterial, such as, say, music or motion. Between the two there are, as would be expected, more shades than easily distinguished distinctions. Speaking of an example of one of these —probably—M. André Lhote, a genuine authority whom it is difficult to refrain from citing at length, observes sympathetically, being himself a painter: "His open window is deformed in a manner which is not in the least arbitrary, and the town gently topples into the room." This, he explains, is in accord with "a formula" he has himself used, "which aims at reconstructing the interior mechanism of sensation." Thus, even since Bergson, it appears, "the mechanistic view" persists.

> "Art still has truth, take refuge there,"

sings Arnold, summing up Goethe. But surely Goethe would have felt the insecurity as a refuge of truth that topples, however gently, and perhaps have decreed it not art at all—at least, not his kind.

Symbolic art has, no doubt, its interest; in any case, the interest of sport conceived as science, or, it may be, science treated as sport. Much of it, to be sure, may recall Johnson's remark on Shenstone's landscape gardening: "Perhaps a sullen and surly spectator may think such performances rather the sport than the business of human reason." There is unquestionably a tendency in the sportiveness of "modern art" to create sullen and surly spectators; and the side of it that produces gloom in the serious makes gaiety in its presence seem ghastly even to the flippant. It is interesting to speculate as to what Muybridge, who saw his discoveries as aids to representation, would think of Matisse, who presents them as a substitute for it: Lot's wife, say, in mid-transformation into her pillar of salt instead of, as we know her, either before or after taking her backward glance, and as only the camera could catch her. Portraying invisible transition, though securing rhythm by falsifying rhyme and reason, destroys the integrity of the dancing lady dislocated for the purpose. She is indeed fatally rhythmic; dance she must since, ceasing, and lacking the wherewithal, she would be unable to sit down. Nature is caricatured out of its concreteness in order to achieve the abstractness of arabesque. The result in this case has a certain rudimentary degree of style, in virtue of rhythmic continuity of line—devitalized, however, by the grotesqueness of its distortion. But the normal relations of style and significant substance are clearly inverted, style, though beautiful in itself, as in arabesque, being an instrument through which substance that has sense acquires beauty also. If she is otherwise meaningless it was hardly worth while to butcher the dancing lady to make an arabesque holiday—aside from the fact that even butchered she does not make a very good arabesque, being, after all, more or less there herself and, so far as she is, being sorrowful to look upon. And there is still less reason to acclaim this sort of thing as the art of the future. M. Marcel Sembat ingeniously settles the question of Matisse by asking us *à brule-pourpoint* whether he has talent or not. Certainly he has talent. But because "Alice in Wonderland" is probably sure of immortality no one ever suggested that its vein marked out the line of subsequent literary development. Of course there is a difference: Alice is inimitable and Matisse is not; but imitability does not, in itself, insure indefinite imitation—at least, imitation widespread and prolonged enough to promise definite adoption. *Many* more Matisses would probably cause a *pre*-impressionist resurrection.

The logical result of scrapping concrete embodiments of imagination, sentiment, beauty, and taste as stale conventionalities and substituting for them materialistic abstractions, as sources of artistic inspiration and targets of technical achievement, has been that the wildest exaggerations are, in fact, saturated with the spirit of the prosaic, the literal, and their derivative, the humorless. Much of the art of the day, fleeing contamination by the conventional, and as terrified at the bogy of beauty as Orestes pursued by the Furies—incidentally a theme handled by Bouguereau in a manner farther beyond its reach than beneath its contempt—or, as Mr. Santayana represents it, vicariously "penitent" for preceding art, has lost touch with the concrete through the confused notion of presenting us with, as I say, stark abstraction of one kind or another as itself a concrete. Thus, it endeavors to represent what, existing only in idea, it is impossible to imagine in form. Obviously, therefore, what if anything it does represent is something else. Essentially this something else is caricature, the well-nigh inevitable bourne both of symbolism intimating the unspecified in cipher without code or key, and of the pursuit of "character" in contempt of beauty. If, too, simplification is an essential antecedent of simplicity with style, its exaggeration is caricature. Avoidance of commonplace that is agreeable, or of even the exceptionally beautiful if familiar, tends inevitably to acceptance of the distorted. Caricature accordingly is prone to enter as an element even into expression that it does not completely characterize. It is, of course, an art in itself that has only recently burst through its limitations in defiance of its own circumscribing principle. This principle in plastic art is the same, I should suppose, that governs the use of irony in letters: the principle that the point of view must be plain, however subtle the treatment. The court to which it appeals must be satisfied as to its identity. Yet in a good deal of "modern art" not only is the public deceived, but the artist himself is apparently deluded and, not voluntarily essaying caricature, functions in unconsciousness of an apparent talent for it.

But the spectator, who is not deceived, finds it no palliation of a mystification that the mystic himself should be mystified, knowing that if he were trained he would be enlightened. That he is not appears not only in the looks of what he produces but in his claim, not that his production is entitled to consideration as an interesting variant (such as, say, "poster art"), but that its proper destiny is to supplant preceding art—as, for instance, electricity has so largely supplanted other power. For him his art, even if ostensibly an aberration, is really the apogee of art—exception being made, perhaps, of that practised by the primitives of his own line of evolution, or of exotic crudities (or refinements for that matter) equally distant from the stage which æsthetic evolution has reached today. To the conservative to have what his traditions and disciplined practice lead him to consider a combination of unconscious caricature and dilettante affectation, exalted above his own production in defiance of his own principles, is exasperatingly incomprehensible. "Amuse yourself with caricature if you like," he feels like adjuring the newcomer in his realm, "but why not appreciate what it is that you are doing? In that way you will do it better. Raffaelli, in inventing the term 'characterist' for himself and his school, certainly did not contemplate *your* succession. But express caricature aside, in the name of rational representative art abandon the delusion of replacing the results of orderly growth by irruptive fantasticalities. Realize that these belong in a class by themselves. As for resurrecting the superseded rather than adapting the surviving past, at least recognize this disposition as a special taste without claims to replace the taste properly belonging to our own day and generation, and neither to a preceding stage of our own, nor to any stage whatever of a wholly different, development." To this one suspects the answer of the "modern" artist would be practically that of the railway official at the ticket window in a French *revue de l'année,* who to the citizen threatening to complain of his insolence, vouchsafed: "All right, complain as much as you like. That's your rôle. It's your rôle to complain and mine to insult you."

So far as style is concerned it is not singular that the simplicity which is the result of simplification should, accordingly, have been so largely overshadowed by the umbrage of "naturalness," flourishing in unadulterated unregeneracy in the garden of art and letters as well as in the surrounding country. On the other hand, "naturalness" being at best but undeveloped personality, there is some confusion in the modernist's psychology. It is certainly not sufficiently recognized by those who, viewing art as pure self-expression, and abandoning its representative function so far as possible, have not merely simplified but systematized and even standardized their simplification, that the order of self-expression they have in mind, being voluntary and determined (and in many cases determinedly like that of someone else), rather than inevitable and inadvertent, is not for that reason more personal. It is, in fact, so disproportionally technical as to suggest the automatic, and even in conception is more common to the crowd of its own practice than was the art of its most conventional forerunners. These wore a decidedly looser garment, and, in the nature of the case, each was more himself, having neither theory nor technic susceptible of such explicit definition and therefore of such concerted exploitation. What M. Lhote proclaims as a "formula" they would have decried as a "trick." They were hard on "tricks." Their own bag of them was not plethoric. Page's "secret of Titian" was notably simple, being merely superimposition, and I remember Winslow Homer saying that about all a pupil could be taught was how to set his palette: "Begin with white and get along down to black." Only as contrasted with absolutely objective representation can modern art, being exhibition of theory rather than manifestation of temperament, be rightly called self-expression. One has only to think of such temperamental variety as within the limits of essentially the same theory the greatest artists have exhibited, to be impressed by the contrasting and astonishing temperamental similarity virtually existing between present-day exponents of all current theories. Tintoretto's painting against the light, and Claude's "setting the sun in the heavens," as Ruskin magnanimously conceded, were not theories of art but temperamental extensions of practice. Temperament, in fact, which would in many cases no doubt justify, is oftenest imperceptible in, "modern art." Yet in the eyes of its adherents it is its main *raison-d'être*. In most cases certainly the self seems to have been absorbed by the "school" it affects, now into a conscious ecstasy of echo, strenuous but essentially academic, now into a harmonious nirvana of identity submerged in sympathetic association. The self, indeed, as subject or source, has largely disappeared and subsists only as agent in this extraordinary theoretic systematization—as part, so to say, of the personnel of the particular creed or craze of which it is a partisan. This order of self-expression, therefore, seems so little truly personal as, equally with that "naturalness" which is altogether unsimplified, to resemble less the pursuit of an ideal than the functioning of an instinct. In a sense, thus, even a cynic about beauty might, if logical, be persuaded that, æsthetically, mankind, revolting from formalism, is becoming brute—*bête*, at any rate, as the untranslatable French word expresses it.

There is, however, one might guess, more future

for the strain in "modern art" which devotes itself to the objective abstract than for that which studies subjective distortion of the concrete to the end of illustrating some notion, itself of possible interest only because thus intricately conveyed. The curiosities of optics can hardly be expected to prove of permanent interest in art; science is too distinctly a different field, and the doctrine of divorcing appearances from reality in order to convey a more vivid sense of it—a blessing brightening as it takes its flight—practically declined into the trituration of symbolism long before current extravagances ran it into the ground. But intensity of scrutiny to the end of sharpening sensibility, in spite of its drawbacks, might very well lead in future to some order of æsthetic system, and finally to a generalizing synthesis infusing with its own spirit the structure of a nature more closely observed, and beauty come into her own again—bringing with her from exile those commanding synthetic forces, imagination and sentiment, in her train. And since abstractions are already in vogue, the cultivation and practice of style should be a short cut to this consummation, style being an abstraction in the interest of beauty, instead of independent of it, being, in fact, itself a potent element of beauty in all art expression.

Existing "modern art," essentially analytic, has no congenital feeling for style. So far as I can recall, it has rarely essayed, not to say achieved, a great—or even a large—picture, has never produced an important piece of elaborate monumental sculpture, has never included a building, properly so-called, among its characteristic edifices; and if it has not it is precisely because its theories prescribe practice in a region where the writs of style do not run and its principles are not considered. Quite specifically, therefore, style, successfully pursued, should ameliorate "modern art" by supplying its helter-skelter of items and episodes with organic order, regularizing the eccentricities of its rhythms, rationalizing its artificial intensities, and elevating its grosser naturalisms, and, in fine, enduing its constructive fragmentariness or unstructural uniformity with enough of its own compositional continuity to create for it a genuinely expressive *ensemble*. And exactly what the selective co-ordinating pressure of style should aid its recovered sentiment and imagination to create is such an *ensemble* as Emerson indicates in his searching observation: "The charming landscape I saw this morning is indubitably made up of some twenty or thirty farms. Miller owns this field, Locke that, and Manning the woodland beyond. But none of them owns the landscape." Fewer fields and more landscape is what lovers of beauty, as distinguished from Miller, Locke, and Manning (naturally partial to the "significant form" rather than the "cosmic effect" of their own meadows and wood-lots!) would be glad to get from "modern art." Nothing valuable would thereby be lost if in this way, and coincidentally with this gain, it sacrificed some of that special appeal which excludes it from general esteem. Such discoveries in nature as attend the practice of art it is the mission of art to popularize, and not to maintain in esoteric mystery. Besides, nature's secrets, like her obvious aspects, are not art until made so, and for this purpose style—being, indeed, that element of art which most distinctly distinguishes it from nature—is an unrivalled alembic.

INDEX

Addison, 80, 83, 113, 117, 132
Adelphi, the London, 65
Aesthetic element, in life and letters, 7; in prose, 82–86, 89, 94 *ff.*, 110, 121 *ff.*; lack of, in modern prose, 142
Aestheticism, 95
Affectation, 40, 105, 106
Albertinelli's "Visitation," 22
"Alice in Wonderland," 208
Angelico, Fra, 51
Apelles, 70
"Apologia," Newman's, 125
Architecture, 98; value of style in, 23; style and manner in, 44; Greek and Gothic, 45
Aristotle, 151, 160
Arnold, Matthew, 10, 17, 108, 127, 175, 188; his criticism, 80, 81; the prose doctrine of, 82–86, 115, 116, 118; his apostrophe to Oxford, 119; simplicity and clarity in style of, 120; his formula of religion, 121; quoted, 33, 52, 76, 93, 95, 104, 125, 126, 150, 160, 166, 206
Art, style the organic factor in, 10, 11; aspiration to achieve perfection in, 16; the secret of creative, 17; likened to a woman by Santayana, 50; critics of, 99–101; the æsthetic element in, 102; simplification in modern, 108; naturalistic tendencies in, 183, 184; relations between life and, 197 *ff.*; the modern movement in, 205 *ff.*; symbolic, 207; the future of, 208, 215–217; caricature in modern, 209–211; temperament in, 214; value of style to modern, 216
Artist, the mind of the, 60
Artistic impulse, the, 17
Asceticism, 95, 183
Asiatic prose, 79, 83
Aspiration, artistic, 16, 17
Association, 32 *ff.*
Atmosphere, 32 *ff.*
Attic prose, 79, 83
Augustan Age, the, 115, 116
Author, the, and his work, 35, 36, 67

Bach, 195
Bacon, 113; quoted, 70–72
Bacon, Josephine Daskam, her "Sons of Sleep," 31
Balzac, quoted, 112
Bartholomé's tomb at Père Lachaise, 20
Bartolommeo, Fra, 22
Beauty, identified with truth by Keats, 7; the element of, in prose, 84, 88, 96, 97; order and movement chief element of, 69–72; modern attitude toward, 205, 209
Beaux-Arts, the, sculpture at, 21
Beerbohm, Max, 34; quoted, 55, 123
Beethoven, 32
Bergson, 206
Bible, the, Donne's sermon on style of, 116
"Biographical History of Philosophy," Lewes's, 65
Bossuet, 119
Bouguereau, 209

INDEX

Bradford, Gamaliel, quoted, 112
Brass, the age of, 171
Brevity, a factor of style, 33
Bright, John, 34
Brooklyn Bridge, the, 106
Browne, Sir Thomas, 112, 113
Browning, Elizabeth Barrett, 133, 136
Browning, Robert, his "Saul," 33
Brunetière, Ferdinand, 29
Buffon, 72; his definition of style, 9 *ff*., 51; misconception of his "style is the man," 42–47, 65
Burke, 80, 83, 93, 118, 128
Butler, Samuel, 95

Candor, present-day, 163, 173
Caricature, in modern art, 209–211
Carlyle, 91; manner and style of, 41, 52–54, 126–128; quoted, 55, 56, 63, 70, 194
Chapu, 21
Characterists, the, 211
Chavannes, Puvis de, 51
Chesterton, 56
"Chromo-civilization," 152
Cicero, 17, 160
Clarendon, 113
Clarity, prose ideal of, 77 *ff*., 88, 96, 97, 103 *ff*., 111, 120, 132
Claude Lorrain, 23, 214
Clemens, Samuel L., 58, 59
Cobb, Frank, 90
Cobbett, 41
Coleridge, 63; quoted, 35
Conduct, effect of mind on, 161
Congreve, 117, 132
Consciousness, present-day, 49
Constraint, of natural impulse, 17
Continuity, the sense of, in rhythm, 31, 32, 125
Criticism, literary, 80, 81; art, 99–101
Culture, development of quality through, 67
Curtis, George William, 93

Daisy Ashford, 192
Dante, 35, 150
Davidson, John, 193
Debussy, 23
"Decline and Fall of the Roman Empire," Gibbon's, 129
Decorum, a civilizing factor, 158; present-day absence of, 175
Definition of style, 3 *ff*., 9 *ff*.
Defoe, 112, 113
Delacroix, 195
Democracy, the ideal of, 168
De Quincey, 126
Dickens, 26; the genius of, 55, 56; facetiousness of, 56–58
Dignity, personal, diminution of, 164 *ff*.; the new, 173–176
Disciplines, need of ideal, 159
Discord, 11
"Discourse," Buffon's, 42, 46
Donatello's "Judith," 22
Donne, 112, 113, 117; quoted, 116
"Dora," Tennyson's, 108
Drama, the, 23, 33, 181, 182, 186, 187
Dryden, 112
Dubois, 21
Dürer, Albert, 70
"Duty of Imitation, The," Brander Matthews's, 195

Eastman, Max, quoted, 195
Eckermann, 67; quoted, 68
Ecstasy, of great literature, 26
Education, 74, 153, 159, 196
Egotism, 76, 77
Eidlitz, Leopold, 106, 109
Elegy, style in, 25, 26
Eliot, George, 188
Emancipation, present-day, 148 *ff*., 155 *ff*., 163 *ff*.; of woman, 156–158
Emerson, 41, 191; quoted, 93, 169, 171, 216
Emotion, 121, 179, 180
Energy and genius, 52

INDEX

English, prose, 84, 92, 111 *ff*.; poetry, 84
Erasmus, 4
"Essays Classical" and "Essays Modern," by F. W. H. Myers, 136
"Essays in Criticism," Arnold's, 119, 120
Exaltation, impersonal, 26
Excess, present-day, 151
"Extemporary Essays," by Maurice Hewlett, 138–141

Faith, decline of, 168, 169, 172
Fèbvre, 182
Feeling, expression of, in prose, 133–137
Fénelon, 10
Fiction, art and life in, 198 *ff*.
Fielding, 201
Fine Arts, the, 97 *ff*.
Fitzgerald, 108
France, Anatole, 87
Francis, 150
Free verse, 88
Freedom, individual, 14
French, academic sculpture, 20; prose, 34, 84, 87; drama, 181; style contrasted with American, 182; fiction, 201, 202
"Futility," Gherardi's, 186

"Gaston de Latour," Pater's, 124
Genius, and energy, 52; personality of, 54
German, prose and poetry, 27
Gherardi's "Futility," 186
Gibbon, æsthetic element in prose of, 128; his devotion to style, 129; quoted, 71, 72
Giotto, 150
Godkin, E. L., 91–94
Goethe, 67–69, 206; quoted, 67
Gothic architecture, 45
Goujon, Jean, 20
Gray, 76
Greek architecture, 45
Guérin, Maurice de, 86

Hall, Fitzedward, 102
Hawthorne, 176
Henderson, W. J., 32
"Henry Esmond," Thackeray's, 201
Henry, Patrick, 152
Herford, Oliver, 145
Herrick, 117
Hewlett, Maurice, 40; his "Extemporary Essays," 138–141; quoted, 41
Homer, Winslow, quoted, 213
Housman's "Last Poems," 25
Howells, quoted, 202
Hudson, 104
Humor, Dickens's, 56–58; Mark Twain's, 58, 59
Hypocrisy, and personal dignity, 164 *ff*., 177

Ideal, artistic impulse toward an, 17–19; the idea of style an, 161, 172
Imitation, value of, 195
Impressionist painting, 205 *ff*.
Impulse, artistic, distinguished from natural, 17
"In Memoriam," Tennyson's, 25
Independence, and personality, 165
Individual expression, 11 *ff*.
Individuality, 64 *ff*., 165

James, Henry, 6, 7, 146, 179; quoted, 5, 88
Johnson, Samuel, 111, 113, 118; quoted, 207
Jonson, Ben, quoted, 194
Josey, Charles Conant, 65
Journalism, 89 *ff*., 174, 187 *ff*.; of Maurice Hewlett, 140, 141
"Judith," Donatello's, 22

Kant, 54
Keats, 33; beauty identified with truth by, 7; quoted, 7, 168

INDEX

Kerr, Philip, 179, 187; quoted, 176
Kinglake, 119
Kingsbury, 94

La Rochefoucauld, 164
"Landlord of the Lion's Head, The," by Howells, 202
Landor, 126
Landormy's "History of Music," quoted, 195
Landscape painting, 88, 104
"Lectures on Translating Homer," Arnold's, 119
Lemaitre, Jules, 29, 30, 63, 201; quoted, 28
Lessing, 3, 62
Lewes's "Biographical History of Philosophy," 65
Lewis, Sinclair, "Main Street," by, 97
Lhote, André, 213; quoted, 206
Life, inner, abandoned for outer, 167 *ff.*, 173, 179; relations between art and, 197 *ff.*
Lincoln, 32, 80
Literature, criticism of, 80, 81; political and economic, 92; naturalistic tendency in, 183, 184. *See also* Prose
Lorrain, Claude, 23, 214
Lowell, 5, 8
Lubbock, Percy, 199; his "Roman Pictures" quoted, 203, 204

Macaulay, 119, 135; the genius of, 130–132
Machen, Arthur, 26
"Madonna del Sacco," Andrea del Sarto's, 22
Magdalen Tower, the, 88
"Main Street," by Sinclair Lewis, 97
Manner, use of the word for "style," 38–40; distinction between style and, 41, 52 *ff.*; and style, 44, 61, 62, 73; and personality, 72
"Marius the Epicurean," Pater's, 122–124
Mark Twain, humor of, 58, 59
Marquis, Don, 175
Matisse, 207, 208
Matthews, Brander, 59; his "Duty of Imitation," 195
Maupassant, Guy de, 28, 62, 179, 203
Mercury, the London, quoted, 154
Meredith, 41
Meynell, Alice, 193
Mignet, François, 39, 40
Mill, John Stuart, 53, 62, 91
Milton, 111–113
Mind, of the artist, 60; effect of, on mind, 161
Monvel, Boutet de, quoted, 20
Movement, and order, 9 *ff.*, 23, 28, 29, 40, 55, 69–72, 75, 79; and rhythm, 30, 31, 158
Murry, Middleton, 197, 198, 202, 204; quoted, 102
Music, 98; spirit of style in, 23
Musset's comedies, 33
Muybridge, 207
Myers, F. W. H., his "Essays Classical" and "Essays Modern," 136–138

Nadelmann, Elie, 108
Nation, the London, quoted, 149
Natural impulse and artistic endeavor, 17; law and "sports," 13; science, 114; distinction between normal and, 143 *ff.*
Naturalism, a substitute for reality, 201, 202
"Naturalness," 143 *ff.*; and personality, 47, 48, 66; and simplicity, 146, 212; art and letters controlled by present-

day ideal of, 167, 170, 183 *ff.*; value of pose and gesture to, 194; and spontaneity, 196
Newman, John Henry, 124, 125
Newspaper, the, writers of, 90–94, 140, 141, 187 *ff.*; loss of authority of, 174
"Newspaper Man, The," by Talcott Williams, 94
Nobility, 26
Nollet, quoted, 43
Normal, the, and the natural, 143 *ff.*; standard of, 197

Ohnet, Georges, 64
Order, organic, 28–31; a first necessity in composition, 30; and movement, 9 *ff.*, 23, 28, 29, 40, 55, 69–72, 75, 79; and measure in character development, 146; lack of, in modern life, 153; benefit of, to present-day conditions, 158, 175

Paderewsky, 61
Page, William, 213
Painting, style in Italian, 21–23; prose and poetry in, 88; modern, 97, 205 *ff.*
Paris, reign of sensation in, 181
Past, the, and the present, 170 *ff.*, 195
Pater, 95; æsthetic prose style of, 121–124; his "Studies in the Renaissance," 121, 122; his "Marius the Epicurean," 122–124
Perfection, aspiration to achieve, 16–18, 160
Personal dignity, and hypocrisy, 164 *ff.*; the new, 173–176
Personality, and naturalness, 47, 48, 66; and style, 51 *ff.*; of genius, 54; interest of, 60; and self-expression, 66; ennoblement of, 67, 68; importance of, in style, 72; development of through discipline, 73, 165, 166; and independence, 165
Philadelphia, 183
Poe, quoted, 14
Poetry, beauty and truth in, 7; style in, 25, 26; German, 27; separation of prose from, 111 *ff.*; the æsthetic element in, 83; English, 84; prose, 84, 89, 120; free verse, 88; modern, 199
Political literature, 89, 90, 92
Poole, 28
Pope, 117
Pose and gesture, 194, 196
Prose, German, 27; French, 34, 84; plea for a richer, 75 *ff.*, 89; simplicity and clarity in, 77 *ff.*, 96, 97, 103 *ff.*, 111, 120; criticism, 80, 81; the æsthetic element in, 82–84, 86, 88, 89, 94 *ff.*, 110, 121 *ff.*; exclusion of, from realm of poetry, 82–87, 111 *ff.*; present-day, without style, 87; poetic quality in, 89, 120; and fellowship with the other arts, 96; sources of inspiration and of guidance in writing, 96; style in, 97, 102 *ff.*; the writers of, 98, 101, 102; the tradition of English, 111 *ff.*; æsthetic distinguished from plain, 121; expression of feeling in, 133–137; lack of æsthetic quality in present-day, 142; the short story, 184; art and life in fiction, 198 *ff.*
Publicity, desire for, 173
Punch, 189

Radicals, of the Victorian Age, 151; of the present day, 152, 155
Raffaelli, 211
Raphael, 68, 69; his "Saint Cecilia," 21, 22; his "Vision of Ezekiel," 22

INDEX

Réclus, Elisée, quoted, 164
Réjane, Madame, 24
Relaxation, 24, 147
Religion, Arnold's formula of, 121
Repression, 49
Rhapsody, prose, 133–137
Rhetoric, 130
Rhythm, 30, 31, 112, 146, 158
Robinson Crusoe, 34
Rodin, 20; quoted, 36, 63
"Roman Pictures," by Percy Lubbock, 203
Rousseauism, 47, 142, 144
Ruskin, 34, 82, 83, 106, 114, 119, 126–128; quoted, 214
Russian drama, 186

"Saint Cecilia," Raphael's, 21, 22
Saint-Gaudens, 107
Sainte-Beuve, 60, 72; "sinuosity" of style of, 30; quoted, 35, 39, 40
Sans Gêne, Madame, 24
Santayana, George, 49, 56, 209; quoted, 50
Sarcey, Francisque, 182
Sarto, Andrea del, his "Madonna del Sacco," 22
"Sartor Resartus," Carlyle's, 53
"Saul," Browning's, 33
Scherer, quoted, 87, 126, 127
Schuyler, Montgomery, 122
Science, natural, 114
Scott, 49
Scriptures, the, Donne's sermon on style of, 116
Sculpture, value of style in, 20, 21; prose of, 88; simplicity in, 108
Sedgwick, Arthur, quoted, 91, 92
Seelye, President, quoted, 93
Self-assertion, 165, 169
Self-culture, 160, 161
Self-expression, 13, 66, 148, 163, 212 *ff.*
Self-forgetfulness, 26
Self-suppression, 14, 163
Sembat, Marcel, 208
Senancour, 10
Sensation, the pursuit of, 176, 179, 180, 184–187, 191–193
Sensibility, development of, 205
Sentiment, 89, 118; decline of, 177–180, 205
Sex, prominence given to, 178
Shakespeare, 194; quoted, 171
Shaw, George Bernard, 95, 96
Shelley, Thompson's eulogy of, 134
Shenstone's landscape gardening, 207
Sheridan, 196
Sherman, Stuart P., 6, 7, 76, 159
Short story, the, 184
Simplicity, prose ideal of, 77 *ff.*, 88, 96, 97, 103 *ff.*, 111, 120, 132; and style, 105–110; and "naturalness," 146, 212
Social unrest, 156
Socrates, 159
"Son at the Front, A," Mrs. Wharton's, 204
"Son of Royal Langbrith, The," by Howells, 202
"Sons of Sleep," Mrs. Bacon's, 31
Spencer, Herbert, 114
Spenser, Edmund, 67
Spontaneity, effect of, secured by study, 196
"Sports," and natural law, 13
Steele, 117, 132
Stephen, Fitzjames, 53
Sterling, John, 109
"Sterling," Carlyle's, 52
Stevenson, Robert Louis, 35, 62, 200
"Studies in the Renaissance," Pater's, 121
Study, achievement of style through, 196
"Study of Celtic Literature, The," Arnold's, 119
Style, a perennial subject of dis-

INDEX

cussion, 1; present-day indifference to, 2, 8, 13, 36, 37, 76, 182, 183, 216; definition of, 3 *ff.*, 9 *ff.*; a universal element, 4; an ultimate æsthetic factor, 5; the informing constituent of the æsthetic element, 8; order and movement of, 9 *ff.*, 28, 40, 55, 69–72; the organic factor in art, 10, 29–31; and individual expression, 11 *ff.*; elevation the effect of, 15, 26; individual freedom not affected by, 14; influence of, on artistic impulse, 18; the art of technic, 19; in sculpture, 20, 21; examples of, in Italian painting, 21–23; the tension of, 24; value of, in art, 24; in poetry, 25, 26; transitions as an element of, 29, 30; vivifying quality of, 28; in the periodic sentence, 27; continuity rhythm's contribution to, 31, 32; association and atmosphere factors of, 32 *ff.*; brevity no bar to, 33; ambiguity in use of the word, 38, 44; use of the word "manner" for, 38–40; distinction between manner and, 41, 52 *ff.*; misconception of Buffon's "style is the man," 42 *ff.*, 65; in architecture, 44, 45; distinguished from personality, 51, 52; not a natural gift, 48, 61, 62, 65, 68, 71; and talent, 63, 64; an element with qualities of its own, 65 *ff.*; ennoblement of self a factor in, 67 *ff.*; beauty endowed with order and movement by, 69–72; acquired through development of personality, 72, 73; simplicity and clarity ideal of prose, 77 *ff.*, 103 *ff.*; fusion of, with manner, 75; in journalism, 92–94; lack of, in modern prose, 87; potentialities of, in the æsthetic field, 97; in prose writing, 97, 102; without sentiment, 118; touched with emotion, 121; poise between substance and, 124; achievement of, through study, 196; beauty acquired by substance through, 208; prosaic because deemed conventional, 154; present-day need of cultivating an ideal of, 143 *ff.*, 166, 172, 175, 180, 192, 193, 197, 215–217; disciplinary use of, 159; the idea of, an ideal, 162; an element of beauty in art expression, 215

Suppression, 163
Swift, 112, 113, 132
Symbolism, 207, 209, 215

Taine, 201
Talent, 63 *ff.*
Taste, tendency to dispense with, 154
Taylor, Jeremy, 113
Technic, style the art of, 19
Temperament, and modern art, 214
Tennyson, his "In Memoriam," 25; his "Dora," 108
Tension of style, the, 24
Teufelsdröckh, 176
Thackeray, 26, 58, 116, 121, 200; style and personality of, 54, 55; æsthetic quality in style of, 132; quoted, 55, 113, 131, 201
Thiers, 119
Thompson, Francis, 134
Thrills, the desire for, 184–187, 193
Thucydides, 160
Tintoretto, 214
Tolerance, universal, 188
Tomlinson, H. M., quoted, 48, 62, 67, 68
Transitions, value of, as an element of style, 29, 30

INDEX

Trevor, Norman, quoted, 181
Truth, identified with beauty, 7

Vice and the new personal dignity, 176, 177
Victorian Age, the, 149–151, 163, 169, 184, 188, 189, 191, 198
"Vision of Ezekiel," Raphael's, 22
"Visitation," Albertinelli's, 22
Voltaire, 112

Walpole, Horace, 72, 130
Ward, Artemus, 163
Ward, Quincy, quoted, 19
Watts, Isaac, 144
Weber and Fields, 189
West, Rebecca, quoted, 63
Wharton, Edith, her "A Son at the Front," 204
Whistler, 99
Wilde, Oscar, 95, 96
"Wilhelm Meister," Carlyle's, 127
Williams, Talcott, 94
Woman, emancipation of, 156–158
Wordsworth, 88, 108; his "Intimations," 160
Writers, prose, 98, 101, 102, 141

Yeats, W. B., 53; quoted, 95, 96, 122, 193

Zola, 201